GW00759016

Arm-Locks
for
All Styles

by
Iain Abernethy

Published by NETH Publishing
In association with Summersdale Publishers Ltd
www.summersdale.com
www.iainabernethy.com

Arm-Locks for All Styles

Copyright © Iain Abernethy 2004

1st Edition

All rights reserved. The right of Iain Abernethy to be identified as the author of this work has been asserted in accordance with the Copyright, Designs and Patents Act of 1988. No part of this book may be reproduced by any means, nor translated into machine language, without the written permission of the publisher.

Published by: NETH Publishing, PO Box 38, Cockermouth, Cumbria, CA13 0GS, United Kingdom.

In association with Summersdale Publishers Ltd, 46 West Street, Chichester, PO19 1RP, United Kingdom.
www.summersdale.com

Cover Illustration and Photographs by Peter Skillen Studio.

Typesetting by NETH Publishing.

Printed and Bound in Great Britain by CPI Bath, Somerset.

A CIP Catalogue record for this book is available from the British Library.

ISBN: 0 9538932 3 5

Important note: The author, publishers and distributors of this book do not accept any responsibility for any prosecutions or proceedings brought or instituted against any person or body as a result of the use or misuse of the information or any techniques described in this book or any loss, injury or damage caused thereby. Some of the techniques and training methods described in this book require high levels of skill and physical fitness. The techniques and methods described within this book must only be practised by those in good health whilst under qualified supervision.

Acknowledgements

I would like to express my gratitude to my Mum and Dad, Andrew and Jill Abernethy, Peter Skillen, Murray Denwood, Fred Moore, Jim Hopkins, Gary Herbert, Craig Strickland, Paul Cartmell, Rob Gate, Doug James and all the instructors and students of Chojinkai, Gordon Harrison, Geoff Thompson, Peter Consterdine and Dawn, Stewart Ferris and all at Summersdale Publishers, Tim and Stuart Eyrl, Roddie Grant and the team at My Word, Dan Redmond, Jeremy Hancock, Carl Steffensen and all at CPI Bath, Paul Clifton and all at Traditional Karate and Combat Magazines, Martyn Goodfellow, Richard Barnes, Tony Mottram, Bob Sykes, Moira Spencer and all at Martial Arts Illustrated magazine, all my former colleagues in LAEMG, and all the martial artists who have so kindly shared their knowledge with me. This book could never have been written and published without your guidance and support.

I'd also like to thank all those who have purchased my previous material, who organised and attended the seminars, who wrote to voice their support, and everyone who has subscribed to my mailing list. Your unwavering support is hugely appreciated.

Above all, I'd like to thank my beautiful wife Helen and our two sons, David and Rhys, for their love, support and all the happiness that they bring me.

Warning

The methods described and demonstrated in this book are potentially dangerous and must not be attempted by anyone unless they are under expert supervision. Any persons attempting any of the activities described in this book do so entirely at their own risk. All readers are encouraged to be aware of, and adhere to, all appropriate laws relating to self-defence.

Contents

Introduction

Arm-locks are found in most of the martial arts. However, the various systems emphasise arm-locks to different degrees. In some systems and schools a wide variety of arm-locks are regularly practised, whereas others may only include a very small number in their training. Hopefully this book will help you to expand your knowledge of arm-locks and introduce you to some locks with which you may not be familiar.

The arm-locks covered in this book originate from a wide range of differing systems. My chosen art has always been traditional karate; however, I count myself lucky that during my twenty-plus years in the martial arts I've had the opportunity to train with practitioners and teachers from many different systems. Within the pages of this book we'll cover arm-locks that are found in traditional karate, judo, kung fu, traditional jujutsu, modern jujutsu, aikido, etc.

There are only a limited number of ways to lock the joints of the arm, and therefore the arm-locks of all martial arts have a great deal in common. However, the various systems emphasise certain arm-locks over others, have varying degrees of sophistication and all have subtly different ways of applying arm-locks. This book is intended to look at arm-locks in general and you will need to consult an expert in any particular system for guidance on the methodology and the preferred techniques of that system.

In this book we will be examining the functional application of arm-locks in live situations. We will cover the core principles, the weaknesses of the joints, safety in training, wrist-locks, elbow-locks, shoulder-locks and transition drills that will help develop the skills needed to flow from one lock to the next. For those who practise a form-based system (karate, taekwondo, tang soo do etc) we will also look at how arm-locks are recorded within the traditional forms.

The arm is made up of three main joints; the shoulder, the elbow and the wrist. Throughout this book we will essentially be looking at the various ways in which the weaknesses of these three joints can be exploited.

The structure of the joints is common to all human beings, and therefore the weaknesses that we wish to exploit are also common. However, the methods used to exploit these weaknesses will vary according to the environment in which the arm-lock is being used.

In sporting martial arts, arm-locks are generally applied in order to get the opponent to 'tap out' and you will be facing a skilled opponent with a similar set of skills to your own. This means that you will need to apply arm-locks in a skilful and subtle way if they are not going to be countered. You can only apply techniques that are permitted by the rules, in a way that is permitted by the rules. The fight is guaranteed to stay one-on-one and take place on a matted area. You will know about the fight weeks in advance and will have prepared accordingly. All of the above will affect the way in which arm-locks are applied in the sporting environment.

In a civilian altercation (self-protection), your first option will be to flee, as opposed to fight for a submission or 'tap out'. If physical conflict can't be avoided, then your aim is to weaken or stun your assailant so that you can run away. An assailant in a self-protection situation is extremely unlikely to be a trained competitor. This lack of formal training makes them no less dangerous as they may have plenty of 'real life' experience. The lack of formal training, and the lack of rules, means that counters, feints etc become an irrelevance as simple directness becomes the order of the day. You can use a wider range of methods because none are 'prohibited' by the rulebook. There is no guarantee that the fight will remain one-on-one and hence strategies that are highly-effective in the competitive arena become extremely dangerous outside that arena (eg deliberately seeking and maintaining a ground-fight).

Some principles are always constant, eg all arm-locks require good leverage, regardless of the environment, but it is important that you understand which environment you are training for and hence which techniques and methodologies are appropriate.

In this book we will be focusing on the use of arm-locks in the civilian environment. Many of the arm-locks covered, or versions of them, are used in competitive martial arts. However, there are a great many additional skills that the competitive martial artist needs that those who don't enter such tournaments do not need. It should also be understood that defeating a highly-conditioned athlete, who has a wide knowledge of combative methods and ranges, requires a skill level way in excess of the skills needed for self-protection.

Additionally, many of the methods used in competitive martial arts are not appropriate for use outside that environment (eg they are sometimes too complex). A highly trained and gifted athlete may be able to make just about any technique work; those who are less gifted should stick to techniques that are simpler and more direct.

From the outset it is important to understand that in a live situation, arm-locks are definitely not 'primary techniques' and fall firmly into the category of 'support techniques'. Because arm-locks are grappling techniques – they require you to hold onto your opponent – they should generally be avoided if at all possible. Your aim should always be to run away the instant you are able to do so. If you and the opponent have latched onto one another, it is no longer possible to run away.

In self-protection situations, striking is generally the preferred method. You should strike the opponent – ideally pre-emptively during the dialogue stages of the altercation – and then flee whilst they are stunned. You should never actively seek to grapple with your assailant. That said, if your initial strikes are unsuccessful there is a strong chance that the opponent will grab you. Some martial arts instructors ignore grappling altogether and simply recommend breaking the opponent's grip and then fleeing, but unfortunately it isn't that simple. Once the opponent has secured a strong grip, it is often extremely difficult to break free. If effective and pragmatic self-protection skills are your aim, you need to possess fundamental grappling skills in order to back up your striking.

Once the fight hits close-range, striking should remain the preferred option. So long as you've trained to develop sufficient impact, striking is very direct and very immediate. A solid strike will weaken or incapacitate the opponent and will give you the opportunity to flee. Grappling techniques generally take longer to apply and require you to remain in close proximity to the opponent. It is for these reasons that striking should be the primary method for self-protection. However, you must understand that striking from outside grappling range and striking from within grappling range are two very different skills. It is a mistake to assume that skill at one distance will automatically lead to skill in the other. You need to ensure that you practise striking from within a clinch and that you possess the basic grappling skills needed to create opportunities for your strikes whilst fighting at close-range.

In addition to striking, you should also aim to use very simple and direct grappling techniques when the fight goes to close-range. Methods such as seizing the groin, attacking the eyes and biting are highly effective and very easy to apply. They can also cause great harm to your opponent and hence you have a legal and moral obligation to ensure that the force used to defend yourself is appropriate and justifiable.

The hierarchy, as we have examined it so far, has been:

- Totally avoid the situation.
- Run away.
- Verbally defuse or dissuade the situation.
- Pre-emptively strike the assailant during the dialogue stages and then instantly flee.
- Strike the opponent until the opportunity to flee is available (avoid latching onto the opponent).
- Strike the opponent from within the clinch and use simple and direct grappling techniques.

If, whilst you are still fighting from the clinch, the opportunity for a more 'formal' grappling technique should present itself, then by all means take it. The opponent may end up perfectly positioned for a throw, lock, choke or strangle, and you could exploit that opportunity and apply the technique. However, you should never be looking for such techniques in the first instance. Take them if they are presented, but be sure to give striking and the simple and direct methods priority. Throws, locks, chokes etc are very much 'support' techniques. The 'primary' methods are striking and the simple techniques we have already discussed. However, the support methods are still very much a vital part of the whole. You need to ensure that you are familiar with all the various methods. After all, a chain is only as strong as its weakest link.

Before we move on to discuss some specific issues surrounding arm-locks, I'd like to quickly discuss the role of ground-fighting. The ground is not somewhere you want to be in a real fight. Becoming involved in a ground-fight makes it much harder to escape due to your vastly reduced mobility. You are also very vulnerable to the kicks of your opponent's accomplices whilst on the floor. In today's society, fights are rarely one-on-one for any length of time. Even 'spectators' to the fight may decide to get involved if they feel they can get away with a 'free shot'. If you are in an isolated area, with no chance of immediate escape, and you are a good ground-fighter, then it could be argued that opting for a ground-fight might be a workable strategy. However, in the vast majority of situations, you don't want to go to the ground. Despite the desire not to go to the ground, you must appreciate that real fights often end up there and therefore you definitely need to possess some ground-fighting skills.

If you should end up on the ground, your immediate aim should be to get back to your feet (see my book '*Throws for Strikers*' for advice on how to do this). Although it is unlikely to be a preferred option, the opponent may present you with the opportunity for an arm-lock during a ground-fight. Should it be safe and appropriate to do so (eg no chance of a third party getting involved), you may decide to exploit that opportunity. However, it must be understood that, in a civilian environment, ground-fighting arm-locks do not play anything like the same role that they do in the sporting environment. We will cover a number of ground-fighting arm-locks in this book, but you must never forget that getting to your feet is always the key strategy if you should find yourself on the ground. In a self-protection situation, you must never actively go to the ground in search of an arm-lock!

Having discussed when we would consider applying arm-locks, we shall now move on to discuss what arm-locks should be used for. In competitive martial arts, arm-locks are primarily used to get the opponent to 'tap-out' and hence forfeit the match (we will look at the use of the tap-system in Chapter Three: Safety in Training). In a self-protection situation, arm-locks should never be used in this way. The opponent may feign defeat or compliance only to continue their assault the instant the lock is released. Don't believe a single word they say! Arm-locks are also very unlikely to work when used as a form of 'pain compliance' in order to restrain an assailant. You may be able to momentarily control their motion, but there is little chance of you restraining an assailant for any significant length of time. To effectively restrain a violent individual, you would need around four or five people to have any chance of success.

In live situations, arm-locks only have two functions. They are either used to injure the joint or to position an opponent for the following technique (often a strike).

Using arm-locks to injure joints can give you a significant advantage as the opponent will then be unable to use the arm in question. However, it's one thing to get a practise partner to 'tap out', but it takes a whole different mindset to actually snap or dislocate a joint.

You should always keep in mind that, in a real fight, the opponent's system will be flooded with adrenaline and hence their pain threshold will be much higher than a partner's in the dojo. That, combined with the fact that you are not trying to get a 'submission', means that locks have to be taken further than they are in training. For the vast majority of people, it is unlikely that the mental resolve needed to snap or dislocate an opponent's joint will come naturally. However, such an action may be required to ensure our safety. We must therefore ensure our training develops that mental resolve.

In a real fight, in addition to the effects of adrenaline, your assailant may also be under the influence of alcohol or drugs. This can further increase their pain threshold. It should therefore be understood that a broken joint may not be an instant fight stopper. Despite the fact that the opponent will have difficulty using the injured joint, they may try to fight on as if nothing has happened! I'm sure we all know of people – perhaps you've done it yourself – who have shrugged off injuries as nothing significant, only to realise later on that they may be more significant than first thought.

The second function of arm-locks is to position the opponent for following techniques. As a lock is applied, the opponent will instinctively move away from the pain caused by the lock in order to protect their joints. This instinctive action takes place without the conscious thought of the opponent (just like when you snatch your hand away from something hot). Arm-locks can be used to exploit this instinctive action and we will cover this further in the following chapter.

To conclude this introduction, I'd like to quickly mention the differing styles of martial arts and the role arm-locks play within them. Many of the arm-locks covered in this book are regularly practised in grappling systems such as judo and jujutsu. However, arm-locks are not techniques that most martial artists associate with systems like karate, taekwondo etc.

In recent years, more and more martial artists are beginning to understand that, to be an effective fighter, you need to be competent at all ranges of combat and all the combative elements. This fact was fully understood by the martial artists of the past. The original versions of most systems were much broader in their scope than the specialised systems they have evolved into. The 'grappling arts' included fundamental striking on their curricula, just as the 'striking arts' included fundamental grappling skills on theirs. It is only in comparatively recent times that the arts have narrowed their focus and become solely about one particular range or skill.

If you practise a grappling art then you are probably already familiar with arm-locks and their methodology. For those who practise a modern 'striking' art, or a modern version of an older system, you may not presently include arm-locks in your practise. However, if you examine the applications of the traditional forms in your system, you are almost sure to find arm-locks. The forms are, after all, a record of the older version of your system. We will discuss how arm-locks are recorded in katas, hyungs and forms in

Chapter Two and you will see many examples throughout this book.

Regardless of which art you practise, all arm-locks have a common set of core principles. It is these core principles that we shall now move on to examine.

Chapter 1

Principles of Arm-Locks

In this chapter we will look at some of the key principles of
arm-locks. There are a number of reasons why it is important
that you have an understanding of these principles.

Firstly, an understanding of the underlying principles will
ensure that your techniques are applied as effectively and
efficiently as possible.

Secondly, knowledge of the principles will allow you to adapt
techniques, in line with the underlying principles, relative to the
exact situation at hand. Therefore, you will be a more versatile
martial artist.

Thirdly, if you understand the principles upon which the
techniques rest, you will find it easier to learn new techniques.
On the surface a new technique may appear quite different to
those already in your repertoire, but it will undoubtedly be based
on the exact same principles with which you are already familiar.
You will also find it easier to adapt methods from other arts into
your own training for the same reason.

Finally, knowledge of these principles will enable to you
recognise them in your forms. Therefore, your understanding of
any forms that you may practise will also be enhanced.

Principles are always more important than the techniques that
they produce. Principles can be applied in an infinite number of
ways, whereas techniques are limited to specific situations. It is
simply impossible to try to learn a technique for every single
specific situation. Because there are an infinite number of possible
situations, you would have to learn an infinite number of
techniques!

Learning many techniques can be harmful as it can lead to the brain 'stalling' whilst it attempts to decide which technique is relevant for any given moment. However, you can learn a small number of principles which can be applied regardless of the exact situation.

As someone who spent many years working as an electrician, I have worked on many vastly different electrical systems, from simple light switches to some of the most advanced computer control systems in Europe. Although these systems may be different, they are all based on the fundamental nature of electricity and the laws that govern its behaviour (Ohm's law, Kirchhoff's laws etc). As an electrician – and someone who trained electricians – I appreciated that the key things to understand are the principles of electricity. That way we effectively understand all electrical systems. Even if we had never worked on a specific system before, we would still be able to maintain it effectively as long as we understood the principles of electricity upon which it is based. As martial artists, we should also endeavour to understand the core principles for similar reasons. If we come across a situation with which we were previously unfamiliar, we will still know what to do so long as we understand the principles.

We will now move on to look at some of the key principles associated with arm-locks. When we get to the chapters on technique, I suggest that you revisit the following section and more closely examine how the techniques covered make use of these core principles. You will find that these concepts seem less 'abstract' when you have seen them in action. In fact, the only way to gain a worthwhile understanding of these concepts is to put them into action. Reading about the principles of arm-locks will increase your understanding of them. However, reading alone will only produce an intellectual understanding. As martial artists we require an intuitive and deep understanding of these principles if we are to be able to apply them freely.

Push / Pull

This principle refers to the two-way motion associated with most joint-locks. Part of the lock will pull the opponent's limb, and another part will push. This will produce a greater force on the opponent's joint than either pulling or pushing alone. A good everyday analogy is that of turning the steering wheel of a car; one hand pushes upward on one side of the wheel, whilst the opposite hand pulls down.

Suppose that I seize the opponent's wrist with one hand and the forearm of my other arm is placed just above the opponent's elbow (see page 54). From here, I would straighten and hyperextend the elbow joint most effectively by pulling on the opponent's wrist as my forearm pushed against the opponent's elbow. Both the push and the pull would help to hyperextend the opponent's arm, and when applied simultaneously their individual effects are multiplied.

To make use of the Push / Pull principle you do not always have to use both hands. A look at bent arm-lock number three (page 94) shows the hand pulling down on the opponent's wrist as the upper part of the arm is raised. This will move the opponent's arm in a circular fashion (a common characteristic of Push / Pull motion) and lock the opponent's shoulder.

The majority of arm-locks make use of the Push / Pull principle and hence it is very important that you become familiar with it and its applications.

Good Leverage

When locking the opponent's joints it is important that you position yourself in a way that gives you the greatest possible leverage. This will maximise the effect of the lock and reduce the amount of strength needed to apply it. The key things that will ensure good leverage are the positioning of the fulcrum (pivot point) and the length of the 'lever'.

Anyone who has ever used a crowbar will fully understand this principle. The closer the end of the crowbar (fulcrum) is to the item to be forced (eg the nails in a floorboard) the greater the effect. Also, the longer the handle of the crowbar, the greater the effect will be. Exactly the same laws of physics apply to joint-locks. For example, when applying a straight arm-lock, the fulcrum should be placed just above the elbow whilst force is applied as near to the opponent's wrist as is possible. Force is also frequently applied directly at the fulcrum point in order to make use of Push / Pull. In this way, we not only get the direct force acting on the elbow joint / fulcrum, but the force being applied at the wrist will also act on the joint and it will be magnified by the levering effect of the forearm.

In the chapter on straight arm-locks, you will see that a body part is always placed just above the opponent's elbow to act as a fulcrum point. You will also notice how force is always applied near the wrist. This gives a 'longer' lever and ensures the force is magnified as much as possible. If we were to move up the forearm towards the elbow, the lever would be effectively 'shorter' and hence the magnifying effect would not be as great. It is vital to keep the lever as long as possible.

The same principle also applies to locks where the arm is bent. You will observe that the force is again applied near the wrist so that the forearm acts as a lever. This is a bit like the turning of a spanner. The greater the length of the spanner handle, the less rotational force is required to move the bolt.

Mechanical Advantage

Mechanical advantage refers to positioning yourself so that you are in a stronger position than the opponent. Shifting your bodyweight is one way in which a mechanical advantage can be gained. As you work your way through the techniques shown in this book, notice how the dropping, lifting and turning of the body plays a key part in the application of the arm-locks.

If you were to try to apply a technique using the strength of the arms alone, your opponent would have a relatively easy time resisting your lock. However, when the body is shifted correctly, your bodyweight will be added to the lock. If your techniques make use of your bodyweight, even opponents who are physically stronger than yourself will find your techniques difficult to resist. A key part in ensuring that you transfer your weight effectively is using correct posture. Kata practise can be a big help with this.

Another way to gain mechanical advantage is to correctly position your limbs. In addition to the correct positioning of the 'fulcrum', and ensuring the 'lever' is as long as possible, it is also important to ensure that your limbs are positioned in other ways that make your techniques as strong as possible. One simple example is to keep your hands as close to your body as the technique in question allows. Your muscles are effectively at their strongest when your limbs are close to your body. Additionally, the closer your hands are to your body, the easier it is to transfer the effects of your body motion to the opponent. Conversely, if the opponent's arms are away from your body, you will have less control over them.

As a simple experiment, extend one of your arms so that it is a short distance from your partner's chest. Then try to keep your arm totally still as your partner pushes your hand in various directions. You'll find that your partner will have little trouble moving your hand. Keep your bodies in the same position and the same distance apart, but move your arm close to your body. Your partner should then reach forward and again try to move your hand. You will now find it much easier to resist your partner's attempts to move your hand. Therefore, one way we can gain mechanical advantage is by moving the opponent's limbs away from them, whilst keeping our own arms close to our body.

You can also gain mechanical advantage on some techniques by positioning your body at an angle to the opponent (this is one reason why many techniques are performed at forty-five and ninety degrees in kata). This exploits the fact that the mechanical and muscular linkages of the arms and torso are most efficient when pushing straight forwards or pulling straight backwards. You will know from your own experience that you can't push out to the side with as much force as you can to the front. Likewise, you can't pull inwards from the side as strongly as you can to the back. As we look at the locks themselves, you'll notice how the opponent's arms are frequently positioned at an angle to their torso in order to give you a mechanical advantage.

Confusion and Distraction

If the opponent is fully aware that a specific technique is being applied, they will be in a better position to resist and counter that technique. It is a general truth that the technique that the opponent doesn't see coming is the one that takes them out of the fight. Whenever the opponent is confused (eg reeling from the effects of a blow) or distracted (overly focused on one aspect or issue and hence vulnerable in other ways) you should attempt to exploit the opponent's weakened mental state. Often confusion and distraction will be 'side effects' of other techniques. For example, you deliver a hard strike to the opponent's jaw in an attempt to knock them out. The opponent is still on their feet, but the blow has interfered with their mental function. If running away is not an option, you could then exploit the opponent's confused state by rapidly applying an appropriate technique.

In addition to being a 'side effect' of other techniques, the other way in which the opponent will become distracted is through your deliberate attempt to distract them. Deliberate attempts to confuse an opponent are best employed in the dialogue stages before an altercation starts; eg telling the opponent that you don't wish to fight – when you are certain that the opponent does – in order to drop their mental guard and create the opening for a pre-emptive strike, which in turn will allow you to flee.

If a situation has gone beyond the dialogue stages and has become a 'fight', you should always aim to defeat the opponent as quickly and directly as possible. Therefore, before we look at some ways in which 'confusion and distraction' can be used 'in fight', it is important to understand that the principle of 'confusion and distraction' must never get in the way of the rapid and direct application of your techniques. Don't concentrate so much on distracting the opponent that you become distracted yourself!

A simple way in which the principle of 'confusion and distraction' can be used during a fight is the immediate pushing of an opponent prior to the pull that was your true intention, and vice-versa. The opponent is likely to resist the initial push by transferring their weight towards you and hence they are unwittingly aiding the following pull.

You may also use 'confusion and distraction' by incorporating shouting, scratching, spitting etc into your techniques. These peripheral actions can distract an opponent and make it easier to apply your technique, but you must use these distractions in such a way that they do not delay or make the actual technique any less direct.

Another way in which 'confusion and distraction' can be employed when applying arm-locks is the rapid progression from one technique to another. This progression may have been intentional, or more likely it will be the result of the opponent thwarting the previous technique. The opponent may have been able to effectively resist a certain lock, but because they are now overly focused on avoiding that specific technique (distracted), they will be vulnerable if you were to quickly switch to another arm-lock. The key to being able to switch from one technique to the next is continuous control.

Continuous Control

If an arm-lock is to be successful, you will need to ensure that you have gained control over the opponent. For many techniques, controlling the arm alone is not sufficient. You must ensure that you have control over the opponent's entire body.

There are essentially two ways to gain control over the opponent's body when fighting; direct control and indirect control.

Direct control refers to a direct holding and securing of the opponent's body so that their movement is limited. For example, if I were to kneel on a floored opponent, my knee is providing direct control over my opponent's body. Placing the legs around or over the opponent will also provide me with direct control if we were fighting on the floor. The arm itself can be directly controlled through grabbing, 'sticking' or both. Grabbing is self-explanatory. Sticking is simply the direct control of the opponent's limbs, without actually seizing them, through a combination of constant contact, pressure and friction. You will see numerous examples of grabbing and sticking as you progress through this book.

For the purposes of this book, indirect control refers to controlling the opponent's body through the application of an arm-lock. The human body is designed to instinctively avoid injury. For example, if you were in danger of being burnt, you will involuntarily move away from the source of the heat before the brain has even consciously registered that heat. In a similar way, when a joint lock is applied, the body will instinctively try to move away from the source of the pain. A good number of the techniques in this book will cause the opponent to drop to their knees or onto the floor. In these instances, the opponent has not been 'thrown' as such. The stimulus was provided and the opponent involuntarily 'threw' themselves to the floor in order to avoid damage to the joint under attack.

In the introduction to this book I referred to the two functions of arm-locks; to damage the joint and to gain control over the opponent's motion. Because this subconscious programming to move away from the source of pain is common to all healthy human beings, it can be used to 'predict' an opponent's most likely movement in order to enhance the accuracy of any following strikes etc.

It is vital that you maintain continuous control over the opponent when fighting. This is especially important when moving from one technique to the next. We will cover this in more detail in the chapter on transition drills.

Attack the Weaknesses of the Joints

In order to lock a joint efficiently, you need to be aware of the structure of the joint and how to exploit the weaknesses of that joint. It is not necessary to have the detailed knowledge of a physician in order to effectively apply arm-locks. The martial artist need only be aware of the basic structure and range of motion that each joint has. This knowledge is useless if your understanding is purely intellectual. To be able to apply this knowledge during a fight, your understanding of these weaknesses needs to progress to be more 'intuitive'.

In this book we will be dealing with locks that attack the wrists, the elbows and the shoulder joints. Although the joints are discussed separately, it is important to understand that many arm-locks make use of the interaction between the joints. For example, some wrist-locks require the elbow to be bent in order to increase the effect of the lock by limiting the rotation of the shoulder. Although reading the following information will help, the best way to understand these interactions and limitations is through the practise of techniques that exploit them.

The Wrist: The wrist is made up of two rows of bones (Carpal bones) and it is held together by four ligaments. The wrist joint itself is the connection of the Radius to the first row of small bones. The wrist joint is very mobile and can move around one-hundred and thirty degrees up and down and sixty degrees side to side. The wrist joint is attacked by moving the hand and forearm outside the permitted range of motion.

The wrist is a relatively small and weak joint and, as such, it is easy to damage. However, because the joint is small, small movements are required to manipulate it. During a live fight the chemicals released into the bloodstream can vastly reduce your fine motor skills. It is for this reason that wrist-locks are nowhere near as effective as they can appear during relaxed and compliant practise.

The wrist is sometimes bent so that the hand can be used as a 'lever' in order to twist the bones of the forearm together (Ulna and Radius). In these instances it is the structure of the elbow joint that is mainly under attack. However, because it is the wrist that is being manipulated, such techniques are most often classified as wrist-locks.

The Elbow: The elbow is made up of the three joints between the Humerus, Ulna and Radius bones. These joints are held together by four main ligaments. The joint of the Ulna and Humerus enables the arm to straighten and bend. The elbow is capable of bending through an angle of around one-hundred and forty degrees. The structure of the elbow joint does not normally allow the forearm to move any further back once the arm is straight, although some individuals do have a slightly greater range of motion. It is this limitation of the elbow joint that is most frequently attacked on straight arm-locks.

The joint of the Ulna and Radius, together with the joint of the Radius and Humerus, allows the forearm to rotate around one-hundred and eighty degrees. Beyond this point the bones of the Ulna and Radius come together and prevent any further movement. This limitation is often attacked through the use of the opponent's hand as a lever in order to twist the bones together.

The Shoulder Joint: The shoulder has the greatest range of motion of all the joints in the human body. The shoulder joint is a ball and socket joint. The 'ball' is the large head of the Humerus bone, and the 'socket' is the shallow Glenoid cavity of the shoulder blade. The ball is larger than the socket and only a small part of the ball is enclosed by the joint. The joint is kept together by three main ligaments (Capsular, Coraco-humeral and

Glenoid). The shoulders are extremely mobile, very unstable joints and are hence quite susceptible to injury.

The shoulder joint allows movement in all directions. However, the most frequently exploited limitation is the clockwise and anticlockwise rotation of the upper arm. Whilst the exact range of motion varies from person to person, there comes a point, in both directions, where the Humerus can't rotate any further. Many of the arm-locks which attack the shoulder joint attempt to twist the Humerus beyond the range of motion permitted by the structure of the joint in order to cause pain, damage the related ligaments and nerves, and control the opponent's movement.

The other limitation of the shoulder that is frequently attacked is the limited backward motion of the Humerus. On the locks where the opponent's forearm is bent up their back (hammer locks etc) it is this limitation that is under attack. By moving the Humerus further backward than the structure of the joint allows we can damage the shoulder joint.

That concludes our look at the key principles associated with arm-locks. To reiterate what was said at the start of this chapter, an intuitive understanding of these principles is needed if you are to be able to use arm-locks effectively and efficiently in live combat. Don't be too concerned if these principles still seem a little abstract at the moment. As martial artists, it is a practical understanding and working knowledge that we require, not an 'academic understanding'. Practicing the techniques covered in subsequent chapters will help you to better understand these principles. It should be remembered that techniques are nothing more than the principles in action.

Chapter 2

The Role of Kata,
Hyungs & Forms

In this chapter we will briefly look at the role of forms in relation to arm-locks. If you're a practitioner of an art that doesn't practise forms, then by all means feel free to skip ahead to the next chapter. Arts such as karate, taekwondo, tang soo do, kung fu etc place a heavy emphasis on forms and they are frequently viewed as being the very foundation of those arts.

Forms essentially exist to fulfil two purposes; to record combative techniques and principles and to provide a means for an individual to practise those techniques and principles. Each form was designed to record what an individual was teaching or had learnt. It would then have been passed on to subsequent generations as a method of preserving that knowledge.

It would be fair to say that it is often the 'striking arts' that place the greater emphasis on solo forms. As we discussed in the introduction, to be a competent martial artist you need to be familiar with all ranges of combat. Whilst striking is the key skill needed for self-protection, a knowledge of fundamental grappling skills is needed in order to back up your strikes in the event of the opponent grabbing you. However, karate, taekwondo, tang soo do, etc rarely include grappling techniques in their practise today. Are we to assume that the founders and forerunners of these arts didn't understand that knowledge of fundamental grappling techniques is required to be effective in combat? The answer to that question is an emphatic, 'No!' The martial artists of the past fully understood the need for skills at all ranges and this is reflected in the forms they created.

All the older arts included both grappling and striking on their curricula (as required for effective fighting), although they rarely placed an equal emphasis on each method. For example, traditional Jujutsu tended to place a heavier emphasis on grappling because the striking of a samurai on a battlefield would be ineffective due to the armour they wore. Karate, on the other hand, placed a heavier emphasis on striking because it was developed and used in a civilian environment.

For reasons too lengthy to go into here, over time many arts began to neglect the 'support elements'. This led to modern 'grappling arts' that only grapple (eg Olympic judo, wrestling etc) and modern 'striking arts' that only strike (eg modern karate, taekwondo, boxing etc). What has compounded the problem is the fact that today's martial artists often have no knowledge of the techniques and methods associated with other ranges. There is an abundance of grappling in the forms, but because many modern strikers have no understanding of such methods they reinterpret the forms so that every move becomes a strike, or a defence against a strike. In many instances, movements that made perfect sense when viewed as grappling techniques are ludicrously ineffective when reinterpreted and blocks and strikes. People then often mistake this 'revised version' for the 'real deal' and hence the reputation of the art suffers.

The forms of most systems are a record of the older version of the art. Hence, through the study of the katas, hyungs etc, we can practise our arts in their broadest and most complete form. As we progress though this book, we will include numerous examples of where the arm-locks being discussed can be found in the various forms. It really doesn't matter if you practise exactly the same forms as I do. These examples are intended to act as food for thought to help you locate similar movements in your own forms. For a detailed discussion on how to analyse your forms I'd refer you to my *Bunkai-Jutsu* book. However, we will now take a very brief look at some of the keys to understanding your forms and the arm-locks recorded within them.

1 - Each form is a stand alone self-protection system.
It is often said that specific forms are for a specific purpose eg defence against a staff etc. However, forms were created to record the full range of fighting techniques and principles. When

analysing forms, be sure not to pigeonhole them and hence limit what you are looking for.

2 – All applications of the forms were designed to end the confrontation instantly.

There is a tendency for forms to be interpreted in an overly defensive way. Many interpretations would have every other movement applied as a block. Each and every movement of a form should endeavour to end the fight there and then. This may mean that the opponent is totally incapacitated (eg unconscious) or left in a very vulnerable position (eg on the floor whilst you are standing). You will notice that many of the arm-locks shown in this book are frequently explained as blocks or non-functioning 'preparations'.

3 – All parts of a movement are significant.

It is vital that you examine the movements of the forms in their entirety if you are to effectively understand their purpose. In particular, 'chambering' and 'preparing' motions are often not analysed in sufficient depth.

4 – Every kata move is designed for use in combat.

We often see movements in forms being explained as exercises to increase strength or improve balance. Certainly, forms are a good way to improve your physical condition, and certain moves do increase strength etc, but that is not their primary purpose. The primary purpose of every movement in a form is to disable an opponent in combat. All movements have direct combative functions.

5 – The angles at which the techniques are performed are important.

You are never changing angles simply to face a new opponent. In the vast majority of situations the opponent will be in front of you. The main exception being surprise attacks, and by definition you won't know they are coming until it is too late! The form is telling you to position yourself at that angle in relation to the opponent. Being at the angle demonstrated by the form will increase the effectiveness of the technique in question. In the last chapter we discussed how being at an angle to your opponent can increase mechanical advantage and hence the effectiveness of your arm-locks.

6 – The stances are a vital component of the techniques.

A key part of effective fighting is ensuring that you use your bodyweight when applying techniques. The stances illustrate the weight distribution and leg position to be utilised during that technique. Remember that the correct use of bodyweight is an important part of ensuring our arm-locks are effective.

7 – Real fights are sloppy affairs and the way the application is performed will reflect this.

The movement in the form represents the ideal. However, real fights are very chaotic and hence you should not expect the movement to remain exactly the same as it appears in the form. Provided the movement is recognisable and is the same in essence, a slight loss of form is a good indicator that you are practising in a realistic manner. Visual appearance is an irrelevance. The effect of the technique is all that matters.

8 – There is a need for skills at every range.

To be a competent martial artist, you need skills at all ranges of combat. Forms are not just striking and blocking drills, they are records of the full range of combative methods. If you've only had exposure to striking methods, then that is all you will see in your forms. This again emphasises the need for your training to be as broad as possible. After reading this book, you should find it much easier to locate arm-locks in your forms.

9 – The likelihood of any attack must be considered.

A common error in martial circles is the misguided assumption that all able fighters will behave like able practitioners of their particular discipline. It is for this reason that the vast majority of books on karate katas show nothing in the way of applications other than 'defences' against 'karate attacks'. In a self-protection situation, your assailant is very unlikely to behave like a martial artist in the dojo or the sporting environment. Forms are not about fighting other martial artists. They are about neutralising the aggression of an attacker, who is highly unlikely to use 'martial arts techniques', in an environment where no etiquette is observed or rules obeyed.

10 – Strikes should be delivered to anatomical weak points.

All the strikes in the forms should be aimed at suitable weak areas of the opponent's anatomy. When analysing your forms you should have a clear idea of which area is under attack. Remember that the forms show the ideal movement. Real fights are intense and frantic affairs and the accurate placement of blows becomes extremely difficult once an altercation is underway. The key thing is to be able to strike the opponent with force. We aim for the weak points that are recorded in the forms, but the reality of combat means that the accurate landing of a blow should be viewed as a bonus. The application of an arm-lock can help to momentarily position an opponent so that an accurate strike is more likely. The forms frequently follow up arm-locks with strikes.

11 – No kata techniques rely upon unpredictable actions from the opponent; however, predictable responses should be acknowledged.

Personally, I dislike any interpretation where your opponent / partner is required to perform certain actions in order to make the technique valid. A good interpretation or technique should require nothing from the opponent. However, there are some responses from the opponent that we can predict (the instinctive way in which the human body moves away from a source of pain). When we apply certain arm-locks the opponent will instinctively try to move away from the lock. Any follow up movements in the forms should acknowledge this involuntary movement from the opponent.

12 – There are many effective applications for every movement.

You will often find that a movement in a form will have more than one effective application. Every one of us is different. It is my belief that everyone must use the forms in a way that works for them. We should all interpret and apply the forms in a way that complements our own strengths and weaknesses. I'm not saying we should radically change the forms; they are generally fine as they are. We should, however, ensure that we apply the techniques and concepts contained within the forms in a way that works for us as individuals.

Contrary to prevailing thought, understanding the forms is not the sole reserve of those who possess 'the secrets'. Everyone can, and should, study the forms for themselves. This will undoubtedly mean that there will be some variations in opinion with regards to how certain movements and concepts should be applied. That is exactly how is should be! If someone interprets the forms in a different way to you, that does not invalidate your interpretation, or theirs.

13 – All applications must be workable in real situations.

It is common sense that a technique must be effective if it is to be deemed valid. However, an understanding of what makes techniques workable is a rarer commodity. It is very common to see the forms interpreted in a way that is overly complex, overly defensive, reliant on a passive or compliant attacker etc. It is vital that students are exposed to the sensations of combat if they are to be able to make informed decisions on what will work and what will not. It is for this reason that I believe the serious martial artist must engage in live, any-range, non-compliant sparring.

It seems blindingly obvious to me that if you wish to learn to fight, then you have to practise fighting. No amount of kata, pad work or drills will give you the required skills if you never progress to practise your techniques against a non-compliant opponent. I've written about this at length in my other books and do not wish to repeat myself here. Suffice to say that if you are to be able to utilise your forms in a real situation, you must practise doing so in a realistic fashion. If you're going to be an able martial artist you need to experience the sensations of 'combat' first hand. In this way your knowledge will be factual, not theoretical. Hence, you'll be in a better position to interpret the forms correctly.

14 – Endeavour to understand the principles upon which the techniques are based.

A form is essentially a record of a fighting system. When constructing the forms, it would make little sense to include every single technique in that system because the form would become impracticably long. A good fighter would understand that principles are much more important than techniques. Hence it would make more sense to record techniques that expressed the key principles of the fighting system.

Forms contain information on strikes, throws, chokes, locks, strangles, holds, groundwork etc. To try to fit all the various techniques into a single form would be impossible. In the last chapter we covered the six key principles that apply to all arm-locks. If the founder of a form wished to record information on arm-locks, their aim would be best served by including a sample of locks that expressed those six key principles, as opposed to trying to record every single arm-lock! I believe that is exactly what the creators of the forms did. So, if a particular form contains only a small number of arm-locks, it does not mean that we should limit our study to those specific locks. We should endeavour to understand the principles upon which those techniques are based, and experiment with the many different ways in which those principles can be applied.

It is hoped that the preceding fourteen points will help you to understand how information is recorded in the forms. As we look at the actual arm-locks themselves, you will be able to directly compare movements in the forms with their applications. This will also help you to further understand these fourteen points and how arm-locks are recorded in the forms.

Some of the arm-locks we will cover may not appear in the forms that you practise. However, the principles on which they are based certainly do! In our training and study we should experiment with the techniques and principles of the forms, not rigidly stick to specific techniques.

An analogy I like to use is to think of a form as being like a block of ice. The shape of the block of ice is constant. However, if heat is added, the ice will turn into water and its shape will adapt to fit its circumstances. Likewise, a form is also constant, but in the heat of combat it will also adapt to its circumstances. The block of ice and the free flowing water may look very different, but they are essentially identical (the same molecules of hydrogen and oxygen). In the same way, a form may look different to the techniques being applied in a live fight, but they are also essentially identical (the same combative principles). It is vital that we learn to freely apply the principles of arm-locks, and exploit the weaknesses of the joints, regardless of the exact situation in which we find ourselves.

One of my favourite quotations in the martial arts is that of Hironori Otsuka (founder of Wado-Ryu karate); '*It is obvious that these kata must be trained and practised sufficiently, but one must not be 'stuck' in them. One must withdraw from the kata to produce forms with no limits or else it becomes useless. It is important to alter the form of the trained kata without hesitation to produce countless other forms of training. Essentially, it is a habit – created over long periods of training. Because it is a habit, it comes to life with no hesitation – by the subconscious mind.*' ('Wado-ryu Karate' page 19-20).

Otsuka is telling us that we should integrate the principles of the forms into our subconscious so that we can freely apply those principles relative to the situation at hand. Again, this emphasises the importance of principles over techniques and tells us that the forms are essentially a record of these key principles.

In addition to adapting the arm-locks of the forms for use in other situations, you should also look at how other arts apply the principles recorded in our forms. All arm-locks are based on the exact same principles, regardless of the art from which they originate. If we can learn a new variation on the techniques of the forms, or a new way of expressing the core principles, we would be foolish to ignore them just because they come from another art.

At the start of this chapter we said that one of the roles of the forms was to record techniques and principles. So if we are to learn new techniques, does that mean we have to create new forms? There is no reason why you couldn't create further forms, but in my opinion there is no real need to do so.

Any 'new' arm-lock is sure to have plenty in common with the techniques already present in your existing forms. All you need to do is 'mentally attach' the new technique to that part of the form. You don't alter the form; simply make a mental note of the 'new variation' of the technique in the form. In the same way that the founder of the form only recorded specific examples to express core principles, you are simply attaching the new technique to that in the form which best demonstrates the principles upon which it is based. This will give you a point of reference and method of recording the technique, which is, after all, one of the key functions of the form. Whilst it is possible that the founder of the form may not have been aware of that specific technique, they were aware of the underlying principles and I feel certain they would welcome their form being used to record these additional methods.

I'm sure there are some who would argue that recording 'non-traditional' techniques using a 'traditional medium' is not acceptable. However, to my mind the 'traditional' function of a form is to record effective techniques and principles. That is exactly what we are doing on the occasions when we 'attach' arm-locks to the form that were derived from other sources.

Although I find the history of the various arts extremely interesting, I'm no historian. I'm first and foremost a pragmatist. Some understanding of the history and development of the forms is important if we are to be able to understand them in their correct context, but we should never let history get in the way of practicalities. Whilst some people may only be interested in the 'original' applications of the form, what really matters to me as a pragmatist is how I can make use of the traditional forms to expand, enhance and record my martial skills. If I sometimes interpret and make use of the forms in a differing way to the martial artists of the past, then so be it. How the martial artists of the past utilised the forms should never be a barrier to our progress. We should avoid restrictive historical dogma and ensure that we remain true to the core tradition of pragmatism. Perhaps paradoxically, I feel certain that it is this approach that the past masters would wish us to adopt. As Otsuka said, we should not become stuck in the katas, but instead make use of them to produce forms with 'no limits.'

Traditional forms have a great deal to offer the martial artist, but only when they are correctly understood, practised and expressed. It is hoped that this chapter has helped you to better understand the nature of forms, how arm-locks are recorded within them, and how we can use traditional forms to help us record arm-locks derived from other sources. The examples in the technical sections of this book will also help to increase your understanding of the arm-locks in the forms.

Before we move onto the next chapter, I will briefly summarise the key points relating to forms:

- Forms exist to record combative techniques and principles, and to provide a method of solo practise.
- Forms record techniques and principles for use at all ranges of combat (strikes, arm-locks, throws, chokes etc). However, forms are commonly misinterpreted as being for use at a single range, normally 'striking range'. In these cases, it is not the art that is lacking, but the interpretation.
- Everyone can, and should, study the forms for themselves. The fourteen points discussed in this chapter will help you to do that.
- If we are to be able to utilise the arm-locks recorded in the forms, we must engage in realistic, non-compliant training. Practising the forms is not enough.
- We can use the forms to record arm-locks derived from other sources / arts because they will be based on the same principles as those in the forms.
- Principles are more important than techniques. We should endeavour to understand the principles expressed by the techniques of the forms, and the infinite ways in which they can be applied.

Chapter 3

Safety in Training

In this chapter we will look at some of the key safety issues associated with practising arm-locks. These techniques have the potential to irreparably damage the joints of the arm and hence great care must be taken in practise. If you don't know how to make your training as safe as possible, your training will not be productive and serious injury is always a possibility. If competence is to be achieved, it is vital that you read, digest and adhere to the information covered in this chapter.

Before we look at the specifics associated with the safe practise of arm-locks, you should remember that the area used for training is of great importance. Be sure that good dojo standards are always adhered to. The training area should be clean, dry, warm, have sufficient space, good ventilation, first aid facilities, a means of contacting emergency services etc.

A vital part of keeping your practise safe is ensuring that all training is supervised by a competent person. This is doubly true if you're relatively inexperienced with arm-locks. Someone with sufficient experience must always oversee the training in order to ensure that it is safe and that the techniques are being correctly applied.

You must also ensure that you and your partner are in good health before engaging in the training methods and techniques described in this book. Of particular importance are any illnesses or injuries that may affect the strength or stability of your joints, bones, ligaments, etc. You are strongly advised to consult a doctor before engaging in any of the activities described in this book.

A number of the techniques covered in this book can result in your partner being taken to the floor. For those techniques you should use suitable mats and perform the technique in a way that allows your partner to land safely. You must also wear additional protective equipment when required eg gloves, knee-pads, gum-shield etc. Exactly what protective equipment is required will depend upon the exact type of practise. The experienced person supervising the training will be able to advise you on the correct protective equipment required for each type of practise.

A competent training partner is vital for productive and safe practise. Your partner will be taking your joints to their natural limit and it is vital that they do not take them even one millimetre further. Training partners who are overly excitable, or whose egos make them take things personally, should always be avoided. What you need are partners who are prepared to work hard, are serious in their approach to their training, have a strong desire to continuously improve, and wish for you to improve also. Certainly, your partners need to give you a demanding and productive training session, but they should not be intentionally trying to injure or 'out do' you.

As you get better, your partners will need to improve. As your partners improve, you will also need to get better. It is in your own interest that your partners improve as much as possible. Training should not be a 'contest' to prove who's the 'best', but a process of mutual improvement. If egos start to rise, training will undoubtedly become more dangerous and less beneficial. The people I've trained with have always been hardworking, dedicated, talented and enthusiastic. When you train with people like these, training is not only safe and productive; it's also a lot of fun.

Control must be exercised when applying all arm-locks. The lock must go on smoothly and gradually. When your partner feels that their joint has reached its natural limit, they should 'tap'. By 'tap' I mean that they should tap your body a few times in rapid succession to indicate that the technique has been successfully applied. The lock should then be instantly released.

In some instances, your positioning may make it difficult for your partner to tap your body. In these instances, your partner should strongly tap the floor and verbally inform you that the technique is 'on'. If both arms are tied, your partner should tap the floor with one of their feet. Again, they should also verbally inform you that the technique is 'on'.

During practise you should always be ready to release a technique the instant you feel a tap, hear a tap, or your partner tells you to do so. You must always be aware that sometimes it can be very difficult for your partner to inform you that a technique is on (particularly during live practise) eg both arms are tied up and their mouth is covered. You should be aware if your partner is in such a position and take appropriate action such as asking the opponent if they are OK, being even gentler with the technique, adjusting your position etc. This possible difficulty in 'tapping out' is one more reason why training must always be closely supervised. The person observing the training should inform both people to stop the instant there is any possibility of injury.

For competence to be achieved, it is vital that you engage in live practise. Compliant practise, although initially important, will not give you the skills needed to deal with a non-compliant opponent. You need to practise your arm-locks realistically if real skill is to be attained.

Arm-locks are not a major part of self-protection; they are only ever used when the ideal opportunity presents itself. Therefore, arm-locks are most realistically practised as part of all-in-sparring. For sparring to be realistic, it must include all ranges of combat and all types of techniques. Participants must be able to kick, punch, grab, throw, choke, lock etc. When you engage in such practise, you must ensure that all appropriate safety precautions are in place. Because such sparring also includes throws, strikes, chokes, strangles etc, in addition to arm-locks, there are many aspects of that type of practise that are outside the scope of this book. For more information on live practise, I'd refer you to Geoff Thompson's superb book '*Animal Day: Pressure testing the martial arts*'. If you study karate, or a similar discipline, you may also like to consult my books '*Karate's Grappling Methods*' and '*Bunkai-Jutsu: The practical application of karate kata*' for details on the safe practise of all-in kata-based sparring.

If your training is to be safe and beneficial, it is vital that you do everything you can to minimise the risk of injury. We will now move on to look at the locks themselves.

Chapter 4

Wrist-Locks

In this section of the book we will look at wrist-locks. The term 'wrist-lock' can sometimes be a slight misnomer because not all of the techniques that carry the label directly exploit the weaknesses of the wrist. Some techniques bend the wrist so that the hand can be used as a lever in order to twist the bones of the forearm together. Certainly, pain is frequently felt at the wrist in these instances, but it is the limitations of the elbow joint that makes these techniques effective. However, one thing that all the techniques covered in this chapter have in common is that the wrist is manipulated to achieve the desired effect.

Wrist-locks can appear spectacularly effective when applied on a compliant practise partner. However, wrist-locks are nowhere near as effective in live situations. During a fight the hands will be 'very mobile' to say the least! This can make locating and securing the wrists very difficult. Another significant difficulty with wrist-locks is the fact that many of them require the fine manipulation of the opponent's hands. The chemicals released into the bloodstream during live combat will vastly reduce your fine motor skills and therefore your ability to manipulate the opponent's hands. Blood, sweat and a noncompliant opponent can also make getting the required grips very difficult. Wrist-locks can have their uses, but they only have a very small and limited role in live situations.

We shall now discuss a number of the more common wrist-locks. Obviously it would not be practical to discuss every possible wrist-lock. However, the locks discussed here will allow us to cover the fundamental concepts of wrist-locking. You will find that all additional wrist-locks are simply variations on these central themes.

For practitioners of arts which have forms, katas or hyungs on their curriculum, we shall also give examples of where some of the techniques discussed can be found in the more common forms. It really does not matter if you practise the same forms as those shown. The examples are meant to act as 'food for thought' in order to help you locate locking techniques in your own forms.

Wrist-Lock 1

The first wrist-lock we shall look at is often the first one taught throughout all the various arts. You have successfully palmed down the opponent's hand (**Figure 1**). Stick to the opponent's arm and quickly direct their hand across and away from their body. At this point your fingers should be around the opponent's wrist and your thumb should be in contact with the back of their hand, just below their knuckles. As the opponent's hand is being moved across, place your other hand directly opposite the hand already in contact with the opponent. At this point, your fingers should be around the wrist and your thumb should be in contact with the back of the opponent's hand (**Figure 2**). Push forwards with your thumbs and pull backward with your fingers in order to bend the

Figure 1

Figure 2

opponent's wrist. At the same time, bring both your hands towards the centre of your body. Be sure to keep your hands quite close to you (**Figure 3**). Continue to move the opponent's hand across your body. Push on the little finger side of their hand and pull on the thumb side. Turn your body as you continue to rotate the opponent's wrist. If the technique has been correctly applied, the opponent will involuntarily move in response to the lock and is very likely to overbalance (**Figure 4**).

At this point I would advise you to revisit the chapter on principles and see if you can identify where all six principles of arm-locking were used during this technique. It is vital that you understand how the principles are being applied in order to make the technique as effective as possible. Having revisited the six principles be sure to look for those principles in action on all the remaining wrist-locks.

Figure 3

Figure 4

Wrist-Lock 2

The opponent is shaking their fist in a threatening manner. Palm the opponent's hand across as you place the palm of your free hand on the back of their hand, near the knuckles of the ring and little finger (**Figure 5**). Tighten your grip on the opponent's wrist as you begin to push on the back of their knuckles. Pull the

Figure 5

grabbing hand in towards you whilst ensuring the other hand remains in contact and continues to push. This will cause the opponent's wrist to bend. Push both hands downward in order to lock the wrist and cause the opponent's legs to bend (**Figure 6**).

You can add more power to this technique by stepping past the opponent as you apply the lock. Project your leg past and to the side of the opponent. Apply the lock as you move your body in the direction of the push and bring your other leg behind and across in order to prevent yourself from losing balance (**Figure 7**).

Figure 6

Figure 7

Example from the forms: Both of these techniques can be found at the start of the form Passai / Bassai-Dai. The first version is the application of the 'opening salutation' (**Form A**) and the second version is the 'reinforced block' (**Form B**).

You'll notice that movements which make perfect sense when viewed as grappling applications often make no sense, or are given no function, in the common interpretation of the form.

Form A   Form B

Wrist-Lock 3

At the start of this chapter we discussed that locating and controlling the opponent's hands during the frenzy of a live fight can make the application of wrist-locks very difficult. In some instances, however, the fact that the opponent has grabbed us helps us to locate and control the hand. In real situations you should never fight defensively or passively. You should always be taking the fight to your opponent until it is over or you can safely run away. We never wait for the opponent to grab us so we can apply our techniques! If, however, the opponent should grab us during the fight, then we may decide to exploit the fact that we now know exactly where the opponent's hand is. This fleeting possibility may lead some to conclude that the opponent grabbing you is a good thing. After all, they are no longer hitting you with that hand and you know exactly where it is. Even so, that hand has also gained control over your movements and can prevent you from fleeing. This can be very bad news, especially if the opponent is armed or they have accomplices. Ideally, the opponent should never secure a grip on you. That said, fights are never 'ideal' and we need to know how to deal with all scenarios.

You attempted to attack the opponent's eyes and they countered by seizing your wrist and moving your hand away from their face

(**Figure 8**). Now that the opponent's hand is located, you now need to gain control. Reach up with your free hand and pin the opponent's seizing hand. If you do not pin the opponent's hand, the following rolling motion can still be used in order to release you from the opponent's grip. Having pinned the opponent's hand, rotate your elbow over the top of their forearm (**Figure 9**). Keep your hands close to you and drop your bodyweight in order to lock the opponent's wrist and cause their legs to bend (**Figure 10**). Secure a grip on the opponent and deliver a hammer-fist strike to their face (**Figure 11**). Wrist-lock three works in exactly the same way if both of the wrists were seized (**Figure 12**).

Figure 8

Figure 9

Figure 10

Figure 11

Figure 12

Example from the forms: This technique is found in Bassai and
Neiseishi / Nijushiho. The lock is applied (**Form C**) and the
follow up strike delivered (**Form D**).

Form C

Form D

Wrist-Lock 4

If you were to attempt to seize the opponent's testicles and the opponent countered by securing a grip on your wrist, this technique could be applied. The opponent has secured a firm grip on your wrist (**Figure 13**). Pin the opponent's hand with your free

hand as you circle your arms around. Cut into the opponent's wrist as you rotate your seized hand and then grab the opponent's forearm (**Figure 14**). Move your hands towards you and down so that the opponent's forearm is rotated. At this point the opponent's elbow should be bent and their fingers should be pointing upward. This will cause the opponent to drop to their knees (**Figure 15**). If the opponent's elbow is higher than their hand, you will be unable to twist the hand correctly. You can rectify this situation by placing your elbow on top of the opponent's elbow and then pushing it back down (**Figure 16**).

Figure 13

Figure 14

Figure 15

Figure 16

Example from the forms: This technique is found at the start of the form Naihanchi / Tekki and is the application of the 'opening salutation' (**Form E**).

Form E

Wrist-Lock 5

Push the opponent's arm downward with your lead arm (**Figure 17**). Maintain contact as you quickly bring your other arm underneath (**Figure 18**). Seize and pull the opponent's wrist as you deliver a palm heel strike (**Figure 19**). Drop your striking arm onto the opponent's arm in order to bend it (**Figure 20**). Push on the opponent's wrist so that their arm is bent around your forearm. Grab your own forearm as you bend the opponent's wrist with your other hand. Pull your arms in towards you so that the opponent's elbow is against your chest. Pull on the opponent's wrist in order to take it beyond its natural range of motion and damage the joint (**Figure 21**). It is relatively easy to take the opponent to the floor from this position. Push the opponent's hand over their shoulder and towards the floor. As you do so, turn your body and sink your bodyweight. The opponent will overbalance and fall to the ground (**Figure 22**).

Figure 17

Figure 18

Figure 19

Place one of your knees on the opponent's head and the other on their torso in order to limit their movement (**Figure 23**). To damage the joint from here, all you need do is keep your knees in position and pull upward on the opponent's hand. This technique is one of the functions of the 'lower X-block' as found in a number of the forms.

Figure 20

Figure 21

Figure 22

Figure 23

Wrist-Lock 6

The opponent has seized your clothing. Drop your forearm onto the opponent's forearm as you deliver an edge of hand strike to their carotid sinus (**Figure 24**). Maintain contact with the opponent's forearm as you slide your arm across so that your

fingers are on the inside of the opponent's elbow. At the same time, bring your striking hand back and grab the opponent's hand. Your thumb should be between the opponent's thumb and index finger. Your fingers should be around the edge of the opponent's hand (**Figure 25**). Shift to a forty-five degree angle and drop your weight onto your rear leg. As you do so, pull the opponent's elbow towards you, bend the opponent's wrist and rotate their hand so that their fingers point upward (**Figure 26**). This will lock the opponent's joints and drop them to their knees. The opponent is then in a good position to be struck (**Figure 27**).

Figure 24

Figure 25

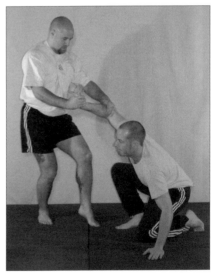

Figure 26

Figure 27

Example from the forms: Practitioners of the form Jion will recognise this technique. The opponent's wrist is locked (**Form F**) and a kick is used to follow up (**Form G**). The lock itself is also one of the applications for the 'double-blocks' found at the start of Gojushiho kata.

Form F

Form G

Wrist-Lock 7

This technique momentarily locks the opponent's wrist in order to release their grip from your forearm. The opponent has secured a grip on your wrist. Hit the opponent with a palm-heel strike (**Figure 28**). Quickly bring your striking arm under the

opponent's arm and place it on top of your wrist. Your arms should be crossed and in contact with one another (**Figure 29**). Pull both arms upwards and towards your stomach. As you do so, rotate your arms so that the thumb side of your fist is uppermost (**Figure 30**). At this point the opponent's wrist will be locked and their arm straight. Thrust both arms upwards in order to strip the opponent's hand from your wrist (**Figure 31**). You are now in a good position to gain control of the opponent's arm.

Figure 28

Figure 29

Figure 30

Example from the forms: This technique is found in Heian Godan / Pinan Godan. Position your arms (**Form H**), lock the opponent's wrist (**Form I**), and finally strip the opponent's grip (**Form J**). The kata then proceeds to lock the opponent's arm, in order to drop their head, before delivering punches to the base of the opponent's skull.

Figure 31

Form H

Form I

Form J

Wrist-Lock 8

If the opponent had secured a grip on your wrist whilst your hands were up, you can strip the opponent's hand by performing the previous technique in the opposite direction. Strike the opponent as before. Bring your striking hand back and place your forearm between your hand and the opponent's wrist (**Figure 32**). Pull your hands downwards in order to lock the opponent's wrist (**Figure 33**). You should then continue the motion in order to strip the opponent's hand from your wrist. This technique appears in a number of forms including Chinto / Gankaku, Kushanku / Kanku-Dai, etc.

Figure 32

Figure 33

Wrist-Lock 9

This technique follows on from one of the straight arm-locks shown in the following chapter (**Figure 34**). Drop your elbow in front of the opponent's elbow joint. Pull inwards with your elbow so that the opponent's arm is clamped to your chest (**Figure 35**). Turn ninety degrees as you rotate the opponent's fingers upwards. This will lock the opponent's joints and drop them to their knees (**Figure 36**). This technique is found towards the start of Passai / Bassai and Kushanku / Kanku-Dai and is followed up by a hammer-fist or open-hand strike depending upon the style.

Figure 34

Figure 35

Figure 36

Wrist-Lock 10

The opponent has seized your clothing. Grab the opponent's hand so that your thumb is between their thumb and index finger and your fingers are wrapped around the edge of their hand. Keep a tight grip on the opponent's hand as you turn your body and

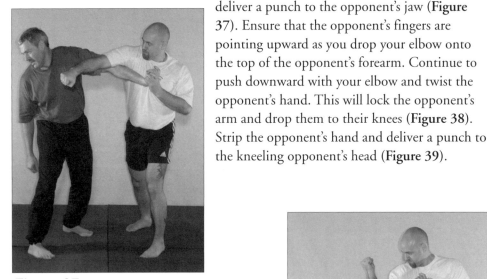

deliver a punch to the opponent's jaw (**Figure 37**). Ensure that the opponent's fingers are pointing upward as you drop your elbow onto the top of the opponent's forearm. Continue to push downward with your elbow and twist the opponent's hand. This will lock the opponent's arm and drop them to their knees (**Figure 38**). Strip the opponent's hand and deliver a punch to the kneeling opponent's head (**Figure 39**).

Figure 37

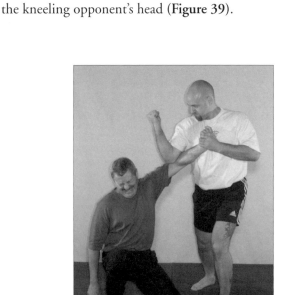

Figure 38

Figure 39

Example from the forms: This technique is found in Passai / Bassai and Kushanku / Kanku-Dai. Position the elbow and lock the opponent's joints (**Form K**). Strip the opponent's grip and strike (**Form L**).

Form K

Form L

Wrist-Lock 11

You have seized the opponent's wrist and elbow (**Figure 40**). Bend the opponent's wrist and elbow as you move to the side (**Figure 41**). Place your bicep on the back of the opponent's upper arm and then place your free hand on the back of the opponent's hand. Pull inwards with both hands to lock the opponent's wrist joint (**Figure 42**).

Figure 40

Figure 41

Figure 42

Chapter 5

Straight Arm-Locks

In this chapter we will look at locks that attack the arms when they are straight. All of these techniques work by attempting to hyper-extend the elbow joint, with the exact method used depending upon what effect is desired. Some of the techniques in this chapter lever the elbow beyond its range of motion in order to break the joint itself. Some of the techniques make impact with the elbow joint in order to reduce or limit the arm's function. Other locks aim to stimulate the opponent's subconscious reaction to pain in order to position them for a strike.

As we progress through the locks in this chapter, you will notice how all of the techniques that rely on leverage to break the joint also have a means of controlling and limiting the opponent's movement. It is vital that the opponent is successfully controlled or they will move away from the technique and all leverage will be lost.

The techniques that make impact with the joint rely on the opponent's inertia. The aim is to cause the joint to move faster than the opponent's body so that the joint becomes hyper-extended. This means that you will need to be sensitive to the opponent's motion in order to apply the techniques correctly. If the opponent was already moving in the direction of your technique, some or all of the effect will be lost.

One key thing to remember about all the locks in this section is that the pressure should be applied just above the elbow joint. When pressure is applied there it will have the greatest effect on the joint itself. When I'm teaching arm-locks, I find that it is often incorrect positioning that causes the student's locks to fail. If you ensure that you're applying pressure to the correct point, your locks will be much more effective.

Straight Arm-Lock 1

During the fight, your arm has clashed with the opponent's arm (**Figure 1**). Maintain contact with the opponent's arm as you slide your arm down and catch their wrist. Pull the opponent's wrist towards you as you place your forearm just above the opponent's

elbow joint (**Figure 2**). Continue to pull the opponent's wrist towards your hip and push against the back of the opponent's elbow. This will hyper-extend the opponent's arm and cause them to involuntarily drop their head to the side (**Figure 3**). Whilst the opponent is distracted and off balance, you should take advantage of the situation and strike them.

Figure 1

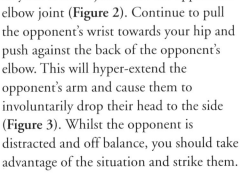

Figure 2

Figure 3

Example from the forms: This technique is one of the main functions of the inward moving 'block' that appears in many forms (**Form A**). The movement is almost useless when applied as a block. It is very difficult to block techniques at close-range, and it is effectively impossible with such a large movement. There isn't anything wrong with the technique itself; the fault lies with its interpretation. You'll also notice how the hand on the hip is actually serving a purpose on the locking application, whereas in the most common 'blocking' interpretation the rear hand is not given a purpose.

Form A

Straight Arm-Lock 2

As on straight arm-lock one, your arms have clashed, you have seized the opponent's wrist and positioned your forearm above their elbow (**Figure 4**). Pull the opponent's hand to your waist as you rotate their forearm. Keep your forearm in contact with the opponent's arm and push down and around in an arcing fashion.

As you rotate the opponent's forearm, the position of their elbow will also rotate. It is for this reason that your pushing arm must move in an arc in order to keep applying pressure to the correct point. This rotation of the arm makes it very difficult for the opponent to resist the lock due to the constantly changing direction of the force. Step around with your back foot in order to add bodyweight to the technique and increase your mechanical advantage (**Figure 5**). Now that the opponent is off balance and their head has dropped down, you should seize the opponent's shoulder and apply a downward pressure. This will ensure that you maintain control over the opponent and it will prevent them from

Figure 4

regaining an upright position. Step forwards and deliver a strike to the base of the opponent's skull (**Figure 6**).

Figure 5

Figure 6

Example from the forms: This lock is found in a great many forms and is frequently misinterpreted as a 'lower-block'. The technique just discussed is found in the karate form Pinan Nidan (Heian Shodan). Move to forty-five degrees and lock the opponent's arm (**Form B**) then step forwards and deliver a strike to the base of the opponent's skull (**Form C**).

Form B

Form C

Straight Arm-Lock 3

Slap the opponent's hand downwards. As
you do so, bring your other hand
underneath the opponent's arm (**Figure** 7).
Seize the opponent's wrist and turn
sideways to the opponent. Raise the
opponent's arm and deliver a hammer-fist
strike to the opponent's groin or floating
ribs (**Figure 8**). Position the bend of your
elbow underneath the opponent's elbow.
Straighten your legs and pull sharply
downward on the opponent's wrist. At the
same time drive upwards with your other
arm to hyper-extend the opponent's elbow
(**Figure 9**).

Figure 7

Figure 8

Figure 9

Example from the forms: This technique is found in the form
Jion. The opponent's wrist has been seized. You lift the opponent's
arm upwards and deliver a hammer-fist strike to their groin or
floating ribs (**Form D**). Straighten your legs and lock the
opponent's arm (**Form E**).

Form D   Form E

Straight Arm-Lock 4

You have seized the opponent's wrist. Slide your hand down and grip the opponent's hand. As you do so, grab the other side of the opponent's hand and begin to turn sideways. Keep your hands close to your body and drop the elbow closest to the opponent (**Figure 10**). Bend the opponent's wrist as you slam your forearm against the back of the opponent's elbow in order to hyper-extend the joint (**Figure 11**). You should then quickly follow up with an appropriate technique.

Figure 10   Figure 11

Example from the forms: This arm-lock is found in the form Seipai (**Form F**).

Form F

Straight Arm-Lock 5

The opponent has seized your clothing. Trap the opponent's hand and deliver a palm-heel strike (**Figure 12**). Grab the opponent's hand with your striking hand ensuring that your thumb is placed between the opponent's thumb and index finger (**Figure 13**). Rotate the opponent's hand as you place your elbow above their elbow joint, turning your body as you do so. Keep your arms close to you as you push downward with your elbow. This will cause the opponent to bend at the waist (**Figure 14**). You should then exploit the opportunity created by the arm-lock and strike the opponent.

Figure 12

Figure 13

Figure 14

Form G

Example from the forms: This technique is found in Pinan / Heian Yodan where it is followed up with a hair pull (often referred to as a 'lower-block') and a simultaneous kick to the opponent's knees (**Form G**).

Straight Arm-Lock 6

You have trapped and seized the opponent's arm. Move to the side and swing your forearm onto the base of the opponent's skull (**Figure 15**). Place your forearm under the opponent's chin and pull backward. This will crank the opponent's neck and help to secure them. Pull the opponent's arm backward so that their elbow joint is hyper-extended across your chest (**Figure 16**). You can then place your hand against the back of your neck to ensure you keep control over the opponent (**Figure 17**).

Figure 15

Figure 16

Figure 17

Example from the forms: This arm-lock can be found towards the end of the form Pinan / Heian Godan (**Form H**).

Form H

Straight Arm-Lock 7

This technique is quite similar to the preceding arm-lock. The opponent's wrist has been seized. Shift to the side and deliver an elbow strike to the base of the opponent's skull (**Figure 18**). Extend your arm in order to turn the opponent's head and crank their neck. At the same time, pull on the opponent's wrist and drop your bodyweight so that their arm is locked across your chest (**Figure 19**). This technique is found in a number of forms and is often mistaken for a 'lower-block to the side'.

Figure 18

Figure 19

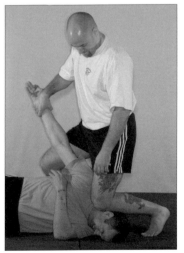

Figure 20

Straight Arm-Lock 8

You have successfully thrown the opponent to the floor and have maintained control over one of their arms. Kneel on the opponent's head in order to control and limit their movement. Your other leg should be close to the opponent's back. Pull on the opponent's wrist so that their arm is barred across your thigh (**Figure 20**). This technique appears in one of the transition drills covered in Chapter Seven.

Example from the forms: This leg position appears in a number of forms and most frequently called 'reverse cat stance' (**Form I**).

Form I

Straight Arm-Lock 9

The opponent has been thrown to the floor and you have maintained control over one of their arms. Place your foot close to the opponent's back so that your knee is just below the opponent's elbow. Pull sharply upwards with both hands (pull slowly in practise) to hyper-extend the opponent's elbow joint (**Figure 21**). This technique is also an application of reverse cat stance.

Figure 21

Straight Arm-Lock 10

The opponent has been thrown to the floor. Position your foot close to the opponent's back. Pull backwards with both arms in order to hyper-extend the opponent's elbow joint across your thigh (**Figure 22**). For this technique to work it is important that the opponent's elbow is just above your thigh.

Figure 22

Example from the forms: This technique is one way in which we can use short cat stance (**Form J**).

Form J

Straight Arm-Lock 11

You have secured the opponent in a scarf hold (**Figure 23**). Secure a grip on the opponent's wrist and quickly change the position of your legs. The foot of your lead leg should be firmly planted on the floor. Keep your weight over the opponent as you lock their elbow across your thigh (**Figure 24**).

Figure 23

Figure 24

Straight Arm-Lock 12

The opponent has been thrown to the floor. Pull sharply upwards on the opponent's arm so that they are lifted and then dropped onto their elbow (**Figure 25**). Deliver a knee strike to the back of the opponent's head in order to stun them. Place your foot in front of the opponent's arm and use your leg to drag their arm backwards. At this point ensure that your other leg is close to your opponent's back (**Figure 26**). Push the opponent's head down and pull backward with your other arm in order to lock the opponent's arm across your thigh (**Figure 27**).

Figure 25

Figure 26

Figure 27

Example from the forms: This technique is found in the form Seishan / Hangetsu (**Form K**).

Form K

Straight Arm-Lock 13

The opponent has seized your clothing. Trap the opponent's grabbing hand and strike them (**Figure 28**). Bring the striking hand back to the opponent's grabbing hand and seize it. Turn your body and take your elbow over the top of the opponent's arm. Be sure to rotate the opponent's arm so that their elbow is pointing upward. Drop your bodyweight and lean backward slightly. At the same time pull up on the opponent's wrist in order to lock the opponent's elbow under your armpit (**Figure 29**). Retain a tight grip on the opponent's wrist as you deliver a hammer-fist strike (**Figure 30**).

Figure 28

Figure 29

Figure 30

Straight Arm-Lock 14

The opponent has grabbed your clothing whilst you are fighting from your knees. Secure the opponent's wrist with both hands as you take your elbow over the top of their arm. Be sure to rotate the opponent's arm so that their elbow is pointing upwards and is under your armpit (**Figure 31**). Pull upward on the opponent's wrist as you drop your bodyweight. The opponent's elbow will be hyper-extended against your armpit (**Figure 32**).

Figure 31

Figure 32

Straight Arm-Lock 15

Seize the opponent's wrist and strike them (**Figure 33**). Put your striking hand just above the opponent's elbow and push downward as you pull their wrist towards your hip (**Figure 34**). Now that the opponent is off balance, deliver an appropriate strike (**Figure 35**).

Figure 33

Figure 34

Figure 35

Example from the forms: This technique is found in Passai kata. Lock the opponent's arm (**Form L**) and then deliver a stamp kick to the inside of their knee (**Form M**).

Form L

Form M

Straight Arm-Lock 16

Having applied the previous lock, instead of striking, take a step backward with your lead foot and continue to turn your body and push down on the opponent's elbow (**Figure 36**). Drop your bodyweight in order to force the opponent onto the floor. Once the opponent is on the floor, pull upward on their wrist whilst pushing downward on their elbow in order to lock and injure the joint (**Figure 37**). Be aware that you are very vulnerable to the strikes of your opponent's accomplices when in this position.

Figure 36

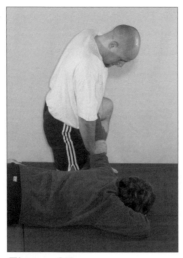

Figure 37

Straight Arm-Lock 17

The opponent has reached around to grab the back of your neck. Drop your weight backward and turn your body. As you do so, push the opponent's hand away from your neck as you slap their elbow in order to hyper-extend the joint (**Figure 38**). Circle your pushing hand to the other side of the opponent's wrist being sure to maintain contact at all times. Grab and rotate the wrist as you push against the elbow joint with your other hand. This will cause the opponent to bend at the waist (**Figure 39**). From here you should exploit the advantage you have created and strike the opponent.

Figure 38

Figure 39

Example from the forms: This technique is found in the form Chinto / Gankaku. Drop back and hyper-extend the opponent's arm (**Form N**). Lock the opponent's arm to position them for a strike (**Form O**).

Form N

Form O

Straight Arm-Lock 18

Seize the opponent's wrist, feed your free arm under their arm and seize the back of the opponent's neck (**Figure 40**). Turn your body to the side as you raise and rotate the opponent's arm. At this point the opponent's elbow joint should be pointing downward. Pull the opponent's arm downward in order to lock their elbow over your own arm (**Figure 41**).

Figure 40

Figure 41

Form P

Example from the forms: This technique is found in the form Naihanchi / Tekki (**Form P**).

Straight Arm-Lock 19

You have slipped to the inside of the opponent's arm with one of your own arms to the outside (**Figure 42**). Clasp your hands together whilst ensuring that your forearm is positioned just above the opponent's elbow joint. The opponent's forearm should be trapped against your neck (**Figure 43**). Pull your hands towards your hip as you turn your body. This motion will momentarily lock the opponent's arm and bring their head forwards (**Figure 44**). Put both hands onto the back of the opponent's head and deliver a knee strike to the opponent's face (**Figure 45**). The arm-lock itself is found towards the beginning of Pinan / Heian Godan and is frequently given no combative function in many interpretations of the form.

Figure 42

Figure 43

Figure 44

Figure 45

Straight Arm-Lock 20

It is also possible to apply the previous lock when fighting on the ground (**Figure 46**). In this instance the lock is being used to injure the joint itself, whereas on the previous technique the lock was being used to position the opponent. This lock also appears in one of the transition drills covered later in this book. In addition to using the forearm to apply leverage, it is also possible to use the hands (**Figure 47**).

Figure 46

Figure 47

Straight Arm-Lock 21

The opponent has got behind you and secured a grip around your waist. Grab one of the opponent's fingers and bend it backward in order to break their grasp. As soon as the opponent's hands are apart, grab their wrist with your other hand (**Figure 48**). Release your grip on the opponent's finger, take your arm around the opponent's arm and grab your own forearm. Be sure that your forearm is positioned just above the opponent's elbow joint. Push down on the opponent's wrist in order to lock the arm (**Figure 49**).

Figure 48

Figure 49

Example from the forms: A version of this technique is found in Seipai kata. The opponent is behind you. Wrap your arm around the opponent's arm and push down on the wrist in order to hyper-extend the opponent's elbow (**Form Q**). Once the lock has done its job, move the opponent's arm out of the way and pivot behind the opponent and deliver a strike to their groin (**Form R**).

Form Q

Form R

Straight Arm-Lock 22

The previous lock can also be used when you are facing the opponent. Slip the opponent's arm and deliver a claw strike to their face (**Figure 50**). Move your striking arm to the opponent's shoulder as your other arm wraps around the opponent's arm and grabs your forearm. Push down on the opponent's shoulder as you raise your forearm in order to apply the lock (**Figure 51**). In order to exploit the advantage you have created, step forwards so that your rear leg is past the opponent's leg and to the outside. Continue to push on the opponent's shoulder as your reap out the opponent's lead leg (**Figure 52**). Use your knee to maintain control over the opponent. Push down on their shoulder as you move your forearm forwards and your shoulder backwards in order to reapply the lock (**Figure 53**).

Figure 50

Figure 51

Figure 52

Figure 53

Straight Arm-Lock 23

Seize the opponent's arm and position yourself for a winding throw (**Figure 54**). Turn your body and pull strongly with your arms so that the opponent is taken over your leg and onto the floor. Although it was not your intention to do so, you have fallen to the ground with the opponent (**Figure 55**). Seize the opponent's wrist with one hand as your other arm wraps around the opponent's arm and takes hold of your forearm. Push on the opponent's wrist and raise your forearm in order to lock the opponent's elbow joint (**Figure 56**).

Figure 54

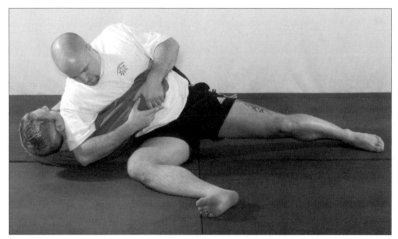

Figure 55

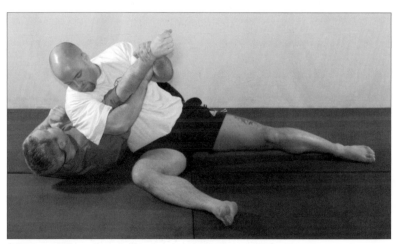

Figure 56

Straight Arm-Lock 24

You are fighting on the floor and have straddled the opponent. In order to protect themselves from your strikes, the opponent has raised their arms in an attempt to cover their head (**Figure** 57). Move your arm to the inside before wrapping your arm around the opponent's arm. Grab your own forearm and push down on the opponent's shoulder. Take your forearm forwards and your shoulder backward in order to lock the opponent's arm (**Figure** 58).

Figure 57

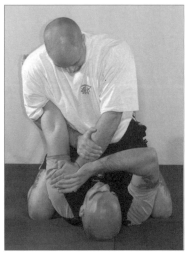

Figure 58

Figure 59

Straight Arm-Lock 25

From the side four-quarter position, take hold of the opponent's wrist. Feed your other arm underneath the opponent's arm and take hold of your own forearm. Straighten the opponent's arm and apply the joint lock as on the preceding techniques (**Figure 59**).

Straight Arm-Lock 26

Seize the opponent's wrist and feed your other arm under their armpit (**Figure 60**). Step round with your lead foot and execute a cross-buttocks throw (**Figures 61 & 62**) (see my book '*Throws for Strikers*' for instruction on this and other throws). Release your grip on the opponent's wrist and feed your arm underneath the opponent's arm. At this point, both of your wrists will be in contact with the opponent's arm, just below their elbow joint. Sharply move your shoulder back as both arms are pushed forward. This will hyper-extend the opponent's elbow joint (**Figure 63**). It is important to push up sharply otherwise the opponent will simply rise with the technique and the lock will have no effect.

Figure 60

Figure 61

Figure 62

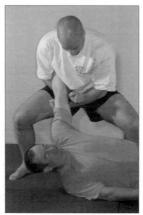

Figure 63

Example from the forms: A version of this technique is found in the form Kushanku / Kanku-Dai. Seize the opponent's wrist and feed your arm underneath the opponent's arm (**Form S**). Execute a cross-buttocks throw. When the throw is applied, you should continue to pull on the opponent's arm after they have landed in order to straighten it for the following lock. This is why the right hand is held high when performing the solo form (**Form T**). Lock the opponent's arm (**Form U**).

Form S

Form T

Form U

Straight Arm-Lock 27

Reach around the back of the opponent's head and take hold of their hair. If the opponent has short hair, you can grab the opponent's ear, nose, or 'fish-hook' their mouth (**Figure 64**). Turn your body and pull the opponent around to the floor (**Figure 65**). Keep control of the opponent's arm, step over their head with your lead foot and crouch down (**Figure 66**).

Figure 64

Figure 65

Figure 66

Drop onto your back, pull on the opponent's wrist and raise your hips to apply the lock. This technique should only ever be considered if the fight was one on one, you're competent on the ground and there was no means of escape. In order for this lock, and the following ones, to work, it is vital that the thumb side of the opponent's hand is uppermost (**Figure 67**).

Figure 67

One of the vulnerabilities of this technique is that your calf is vulnerable to being bitten. The lock will not work if you were to remove the leg, or swap the position of the legs, as the opponent's head will no longer be controlled and they will find it very easy to escape. The best way to avoid being bitten is to first kick the opponent in the face (**Figure 68**).

Figure 68

Push the opponent's face to one side with your foot and apply the lock as before. To gain additional control over the opponent, you can extend your other leg over the opponent's chest (**Figure 69**). You should then instantly return to a standing position. Remember that in live situations you are not looking for a submission, but to injure the joint itself.

Figure 69

Example from the forms: This lock is found in Wanshu / Enpi kata. Grab the opponent's hair, turn and take them to the floor (**Form V**). Hitch forwards and apply the lock (**Form W**). In the kata the lock is shown in a vertical position, whereas in application it is applied in a horizontal position.

Form V

Form W

The idea of using crane stance in this way was suggested to me by a training partner long after I'd actually learnt the lock itself. It may be that Wanshu (the Chinese martial artist whose methods are recorded in the form) never intended for the movement to be used in a horizontal position. However, the interpretation certainly fits the form and has proved to be a useful way to record and mentally rehearse this arm-lock.

Straight Arm-Lock 28

There are many different ways to get into the position required for the previous lock, and a skilled grappler could probably write an entire book on that subject alone. For our purposes, we will look at two further examples. You have gained control over the opponent's arm and delivered an open hand strike to their face (**Figure 70**). Push the opponent's face towards the floor as you turn to the side (**Figure 71**). Sit back, keeping your hips as close as possible to the opponent, and interlock your ankles. Pull on the opponent's wrist and lift your hips to lock their arm (**Figure 72**). It is important to remember that the purpose of this lock in live situations is to damage the joint, as opposed to getting the opponent to tap out. Once the lock has taken effect it should be instantly released. If the opponent should attempt to bite you, kick the opponent and press down with your foot as before.

Figure 70

Figure 71

Figure 72

In sport grappling, it is very common for participants to grab their own hand, arm or gi in order to prevent the arm from being extended. It is very doubtful that this will happen in a self-defence situation as you are facing a different type of opponent in a different environment. However, in the unlikely event that the opponent does grab their arm, you may decide to hook one arm through and use your free arm to attack the opponent's face with either strikes or gouges (**Figure 73**). To prevent these attacks the opponent will need to release their grip. If they should do so, you can drop back and apply the lock as before. If they do not release their grip, you can continue to attack their face. However, it is important to remember that you are vulnerable to being bitten whilst in this position and that you don't want to remain on the floor if the other people could get involved in the fight.

In the sporting environment, attacking the face in this fashion is outlawed. The opponent's grip on their own arm will also be skillfully applied and hence much harder to break. For civilian self-protection purposes – where the opponent is unlikely to be a skilled grappler and the actions of both parties are not bound by any rules – simplicity is the order of the day.

Figure 73

Straight Arm-Lock 29

You are fighting from your back and the opponent is positioned between your legs. Seize the opponent's wrist and move your other arm to the inside of the opponent's thigh (**Figure 74**). Use your arm to help you pivot on your back as you take your leg over the opponent's head (**Figure 75**). Maintain control over the opponent's arm as you use your legs to push the opponent onto their back (**Figure 76**). Drop backward, pull on the opponent's wrist and lift your hips in order to lock the opponent's elbow joint (**Figure 77**).

Figure 74

Figure 75

Figure 76

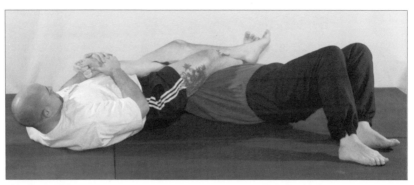

Figure 77

Chapter 6

Bent Arm-Locks

In this chapter we will be looking at arm-locks that are applied when the opponent's arm is bent. Whereas straight arm-locks predominately attack the elbow joint, bent arm-locks tend to manipulate the weaknesses of the shoulder joint. As we covered in Chapter One, it is the limited backward movement and rotation of the Humerus that is exploited on bent arm-locks.

As with all the previous locks, it is vital that the underlying principles covered earlier in this book are understood and adhered to if your locks are going to be as effective as possible.

Bent Arm-Lock 1

You have checked and controlled the opponent's arm. Position your other arm to the outside of the opponent's arm (**Figure 1**). Push the opponent's forearm backward and down as your other arm pulls the opponent's elbow towards you. This will bend the opponent's arm and twist their Humerus beyond its natural range of motion (**Figure 2**). Now that the lock is securely applied, keep your arms close to your body and turn in order to cause the opponent to overbalance (**Figure 3**).

Figure 1

Figure 2

Figure 3

Form A

Form B

Example from the forms: This arm-lock is found in the first and second sequences of the first Pinan / Heian kata. This form is often the second form taught in many schools of Japanese, Okinawan and Korean karate. Therefore, it is frequently relabelled as the second form of the series. However, it was originally designated as the first form of the group. The original order reflects the logical progression of the fighting methods recorded within the series, whereas the modern revised order reflects the technical difficulty of the solo performances.

Check the opponent's arm and position your arm for the lock (**Form A**). Push the opponent's forearm down and back as their elbow is pulled towards you. This will lock the opponent's shoulder joint (**Form B**).

Bent Arm-Lock 2

You have seized the opponent's wrist and pushed their hand backward and to the side (**Figure 4**). Step past the opponent as you feed your arm under the opponent's arm. Grab the opponent's wrist so that your thumbs are towards you (**Figure 5**). Keep the opponent's elbow close to your chest as you pull downwards with both hands. The movement will twist the opponent's Humerus beyond its natural range of motion and is likely to cause the opponent to overbalance (**Figure 6**).

Figure 4

Figure 5

Figure 6

Bent Arm-Lock 3

During the fight, your forearm has come into contact with the opponent's (**Figure 7**). Maintain contact with the opponent's arm as you slide your hand back and seize the opponent's wrist. The instant your grip is secure, feed your free arm under the opponent's arm (**Figure 8**). Bend the opponent's arm as on bent arm-lock one before releasing your grip with one hand as you hook the opponent's wrist with the other hand. Move the opponent's wrist downward as you lift their elbow. This will rotate the opponent's Humerus, lock their shoulder and take the opponent off balance (**Figure 9**). You can use your free hand to strike the opponent on their way down (**Figure 10**).

Figure 7

Figure 8

Figure 9

Figure 10

Bent Arm-Lock 4

You have secured your opponent in the scarf hold. Grab the opponent's forearm and push their arm over your thigh. As you do so, straighten your leg so that the opponent's wrist can be pushed to the floor (**Figure 11**). Bend your leg so that the opponent's forearm is trapped between your calf and thigh. Once your leg is in position, hook your shin behind the knee of your other leg. Your free hand can be used to attack the opponent's face from this position. Move forwards slightly so that your weight is shifted towards your lead knee. This will rotate the opponent's arm and lock the shoulder joint (**Figure 12**).

Figure 11

Figure 12

Bent Arm-Lock 5

During the dialogue stage of the altercation, the opponent has managed to secure both your wrists (**Figure 13**). Rotate your right hand so that the gap between the opponent's thumb and fingers is upwards. Use your left hand to slap the inside of the opponent's

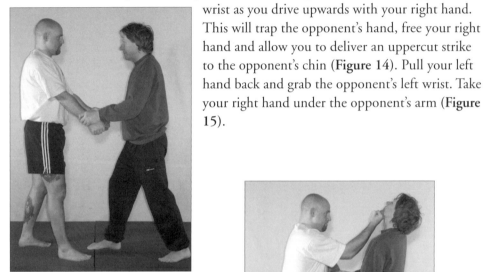

wrist as you drive upwards with your right hand. This will trap the opponent's hand, free your right hand and allow you to deliver an uppercut strike to the opponent's chin (**Figure 14**). Pull your left hand back and grab the opponent's left wrist. Take your right hand under the opponent's arm (**Figure 15**).

Figure 13

Figure 14

Figure 15

Take your feet towards the opponent and execute a shoulder throw (**Figure 16**). As soon as the opponent is on the floor, wrap your arm around your opponent's arm. Cut into the opponent's elbow with your forearm in order to bend their arm (**Figure 17**). Trap the opponent's arm under your armpit. Place your right hand on the opponent's upper arm, just below their elbow joint. Grab the wrist of your right hand with your left hand. This grip will lock the opponent's arm into position (**Figure 18**). Take your right leg over the opponent's body. Turn your body ninety-degrees to twist the opponent's Humerus outside its natural range of motion. The position of your legs will prevent the opponent from shuffling around and alleviating the pressure (**Figure 19**).

Figure 16

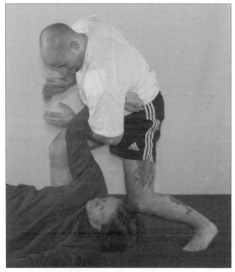

Figure 17

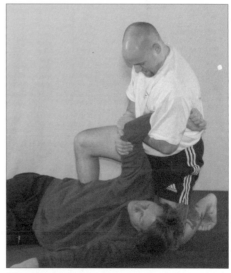

Figure 18

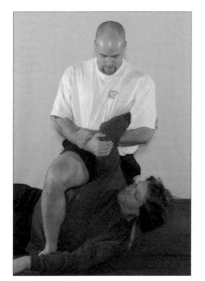

Figure 19

Form C

Example from the forms: This arm-lock is found in Pinan / Heian Godan. Trap the opponent's arms and deliver and uppercut punch to their chin (**Form C**). Control the opponent's arm and then throw them (**Form D**). Cross your arms, taking your left arm under the opponent's arm, and execute the arm-lock shown in figure nineteen (**Form E**).

Form D

Form E

Bent Arm-Lock 6

From the side-four-quarter hold, seize the opponent's wrist and push it towards the ground. Feed your other arm underneath the opponent's upper arm and grab hold of your own wrist (**Figure 20**). Pull the opponent's arm in towards their body and then rotate their arm in order to lock their shoulder joint (**Figure 21**).

Figure 20

Figure 21

Bent Arm-Lock 7

It is also possible to lock the opponent's shoulder when the opponent's arm is pointing in the other direction. From the side-four-quarter position, seize the opponent's wrist, feed your other arm underneath the opponent's arm and seize your own wrist (**Figure 22**). Slide your right knee under your left leg and turn onto your side. Push on the opponent's wrist so that their Humerus is rotated and their shoulder locked (**Figure 23**).

Figure 22

Figure 23

Bent Arm-Lock 8

From the mount position, seize one of the opponent's wrists and push it towards the ground. Feed your other arm under the opponent's upper arm and grab your own wrist (**Figure 24**). Pull the opponent's arm in towards their body, raise their elbow and rotate their arm in order to lock their shoulder joint (**Figure 25**).

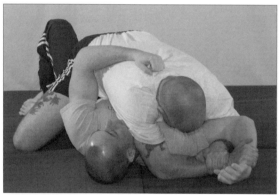

Figure 24

Figure 25

Bent Arm-Lock 9

The opponent has seized your wrist in order to prevent you delivering a low attack (**Figure 26**). Reach across and seize your opponent's elbow (**Figure 27**). Rotate your seized arm upwards as you pull the opponent's elbow towards you (**Figure 28**).

Straighten your legs, pull down on the opponent's wrist and push up on their elbow. This will lock the opponent's shoulder (**Figure 29**). Turn ninety-degrees, whilst continuing to rotate the opponent's arm, in order to force the opponent onto the floor (**Figure 30**).

Figure 26

Figure 27

Figure 28

Figure 29

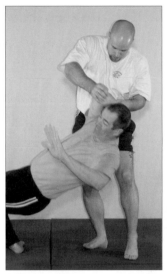

Figure 30

Example from the forms: This arm-lock is found in Pinan / Heian Sandan. Rotate your seized arm and pull the opponent's elbow towards you (**Form F**). Straighten your legs, push up on the opponent's elbow and pull their wrist downward in order to lock their shoulder (**Form G**). The first seven moves of this form map out the various initial grips and ways of applying this lock (see Volume One of the *Bunkai-Jutsu* videos for further details).

Form F

Form G

Bent Arm-Lock 10

To apply this technique your arm needs to be on the inside of the opponent's arm. In this instance, a shovel-hook has been checked (**Figure 31**). Position your arm on the inside of the opponent's elbow (**Figure 32**). Move behind your opponent and push upward with your elbow as you cut into the opponent's elbow with your hand. This will bend the opponent's arm up their back (**Figure 33**). Feed your other arm across your opponent's neck. Pull the opponent towards you and apply a chokehold as you push the opponent's arm further up their back (**Figure 34**). This arm-lock can also be used if the opponent is face down on the floor (**Figure 35**). This version of the technique is used in one of the transition drills covered in Chapter Seven.

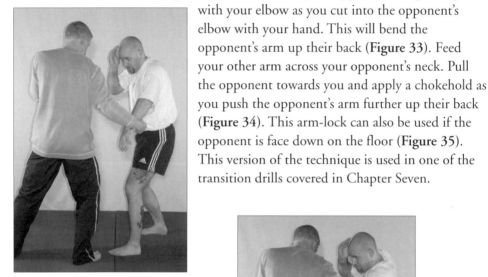

Figure 31

Figure 32

Figure 33

Figure 34

Figure 35

Form H

Example from the forms: This technique is found in Rohai Shodan kata. The simultaneous arm-lock and choke following the one-hundred and eighty degree turn is frequently not attributed any function (**Form H**).

Bent Arm-Lock 11

Bend the opponent's arm up their back as per the previous technique (**Figure 36**). Grab the opponent's wrist with your free hand before grabbing the wrist of that hand with your other hand. Pull the opponent's arm away from their back and towards their

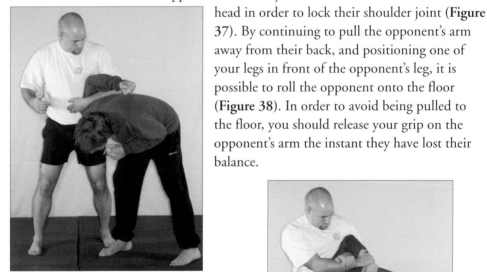

head in order to lock their shoulder joint (**Figure 37**). By continuing to pull the opponent's arm away from their back, and positioning one of your legs in front of the opponent's leg, it is possible to roll the opponent onto the floor (**Figure 38**). In order to avoid being pulled to the floor, you should release your grip on the opponent's arm the instant they have lost their balance.

Figure 36

Figure 37

Figure 38

Bent Arm-Lock 12

You are on your back and have your legs wrapped around your
opponent. The opponent is delivering punches and you are using
your arms to cover your head (**Figure 39**). Use your legs to
sharply pull the opponent towards you. There is a good chance
that the opponent will instinctively put their hands on the floor
to arrest their forward motion (**Figure 40**).

Figure 39

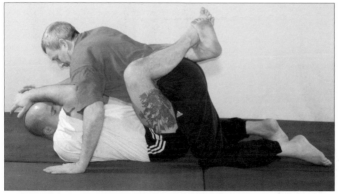

Figure 40

Grab one of their wrists and push their arm backwards (**Figure 41**). Sit up to one side and feed your arm around the opponent's arm and onto your own wrist (**Figure 42**). Turn to one side and push the opponent's arm behind and away from their back. Keep your leg across your opponent's back in order to prevent them from forward-rolling out of the lock (**Figure 43**). You can also use this lock should the opponent try to remove your legs from around their waist by pushing down on your knees. You can then grab the opponent's wrist, push it backward and apply the lock as before.

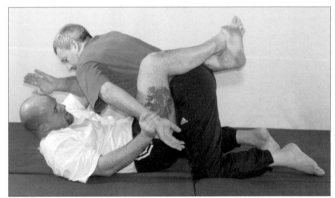

Figure 41

Figure 42

Figure 43

Bent Arm-Lock 13

This technique appears in one of the transition drills covered in Chapter Seven. The opponent is facedown and one of your legs is across their back (**Figure 44**). Bend the opponent's arm across your thigh as you turn your body and lean forwards. The opponent's arm should be trapped between your thigh and chest. Place one of your hands on the other side of the opponent's body (**Figure 45**). Lean forwards and lift your hips in order to lock the opponent's shoulder (**Figure 46**).

Figure 44

Figure 45

Figure 46

Bent Arm-Lock 14

You have seized the opponent's wrist and delivered a claw-hand strike to their face (**Figure** 47). Move to the opponent's side. Retract your striking arm, take it over the top of the opponent's arm, and rotate your arm to bend and raise the opponent's elbow (**Figure** 48). Bring your forearm towards your opponent's shoulder. This motion will trap the opponent's forearm against your chest. The Humerus will now be rotated beyond its natural range of motion (**Figure** 49).

Figure 47

Figure 48

Figure 49

Example from the forms: This arm-lock is found in the form Bassai-Dai / Passai. Seize the opponent's wrist, turn ninety-degrees and rotate your arm in order to bend the opponent's elbow (**Form I**). Bring your forearm up towards the opponent's shoulder in order to lock their shoulder joint (**From J**).

Form I

Form J

Chapter 7

Transition Drills

In this chapter we look at some partner drills which can help develop your ability to utilise arm-locks and flow from one technique to the next. However, it is important that you understand that compliant drills, although useful, won't develop real skill on their own. Live practise is the only thing that will develop your ability to use arm-locks in live situations. In a real situation, the opponent will not be compliant, nor will you know exactly what is coming next. Real situations are constantly changing, spontaneous and chaotic affairs. Drills are, by very definition, fixed routines and hence they will not give you the skills needed for live combat. It is only live, non-compliant sparring that will develop real combative skill. I'm not saying that drills don't have a part to play, but they are very much a step along the way rather than the required destination.

Having learnt to apply the arm-locks covered in this book with a compliant training partner, the next stage is to learn to apply those locks in a more fluid way and to be able to integrate arm-locks with other techniques. The drills covered in this chapter are designed to help you flow from technique to technique, whilst maintaining a dominant position, and to integrate arm-locks with other techniques. I'll stress again that no matter how competent you become at these or any other drills, it is only through engaging in non-compliant sparring that you will develop the skills needed for live situations. Because arm-locks fall into the category of 'support techniques', any-range, 'anything-goes' sparring is the best way to develop your ability to apply arm-locks. All-in-sparring involves strikes, chokes, throws, takedowns, holds etc, and therefore it is beyond the scope of this book (see *Karate's Grappling Methods* or *Bunkai-Jutsu*).

The particular drills covered in this chapter were selected because they contain a good number of the locks covered in this book. These drills were developed by me, they have no historical value, and therefore there is no reason to preserve them as presented here. Their only value is in their ability to act as a bridge between single techniques and the flowing application of multiple techniques. Every one of us is an individual with unique strengths and weaknesses. You are therefore encouraged to adapt these drills to suit your own needs and objectives. You may even decide to abandon these drills altogether and create new ones of your own.

The first drill we will look at was specifically designed to address the issue of arm-locks. We will only show the drill on one side, but it is important to ensure that you practise it on both sides. The drill contains both positioning and destructive locks, and exploits the limitations of all three joints (wrist, elbow and shoulder). You will notice that the drill demands nothing from your partner. I personally dislike drills that demand that the opponent perform certain actions. My reason being that we should not be relying upon the opponent performing certain actions in order to make our techniques valid. I also feel that we should not give the opponent any opportunities and once an advantage has been gained we should ensure that we maintain it. In a real situation, we should always ensure that we fight in a dominating way and never attempt to fight reactively. It is my belief that the drills and training methods we use should reflect this vitally important combative principle.

Transition Drill 1

Your partner begins to move towards you whilst shaking their fist in an intimidating fashion (**Figure 1**). Slap the opponent's hand downward, ensuring that you maintain contact. As you do so, feed your other arm under your partner's arm in preparation for the following wrist grab (**Figure 2**). Shift your body forwards, seize your partner's wrist and place your forearm just above your partner's elbow joint (**Figure 3**). Pull on your partner's wrist and push against their elbow joint. This will lock your partner's elbow and cause their head to drop to one side (**Figure 4**).

Figure 1

Figure 2

Figure 3

Figure 4

Maintain your grip on their wrist as your other arm delivers a palm-heel strike to the base of your partner's skull (**Figure 5**). Bring your striking arm to the inside of your partner's elbow joint and bend their arm around your forearm (**Figure 6**). Grip your own forearm and secure your partner's elbow against your chest as you apply a standing wrist-lock (**Figure 7**). Turn your body as you push your partner's wrist towards the floor. Be sure to keep your partner's arm close to your body and your grip as tight as possible (**Figure 8**).

Figure 5

Figure 6

Figure 7

Figure 8

Control your partner by placing your knees on their head and chest. Pull upward on your partner's wrist to apply a wrist-lock (**Figure 9**). Grab your partner's wrist and turn your body ninety-degrees. Kneel on your partner's head as you lock their elbow across your thigh (**Figure 10**). Use your free hand to indicate an open-handed slap to your partner's face (**Figure 11**). Step across your partner's body, drop your hips and secure a tight hold on your partner's wrist with both hands (**Figure 12**).

Figure 9

Figure 10

Figure 11

Figure 12

Drop backward, interlock your ankles and raise your hips to lock your partner's elbow (**Figure 13**). Raise your leg and indicate a dropping kick to your partner's face (**Figure 14**). You can then push down with the sole of your kicking foot, raise your hips and once again lock your partner's arm. Because you are on your back and your vision can be a little obscured, it can be quite difficult to control this kick. When practising this drill at speed, it is advised that you kick well above your partner's head in order to avoid injury. Having indicated the kick, gently place your foot back onto your partner's face to reapply the lock as mentioned previously. Take your foot off your partner's face as your other foot is hooked behind their neck (**Figure 15**).

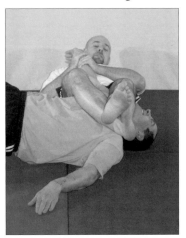

Figure 13

Figure 14

Figure 15

Use your leg to raise your partner's head off the ground. Be sure to maintain control of the opponent's arm (**Figure 16**). If this were a live situation, it is likely that the opponent would attempt to sit up the instant your foot was removed from their face. In that instance, your foot is merely directing the opponent's energy as opposed to physically lifting them. Continue to direct your partner with your foot as you pivot on your hips. Your partner will end up face down on the floor. As your partner lands, sit up straight and position your partner's forearm on your shoulder. Place your forearm just below your partner's elbow joint, grab your hand and pull your forearm towards you. This will lock your partner's elbow joint (**Figure 17**).

Figure 16

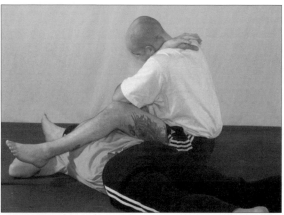

Figure 17

Push down on your partner's wrist in order to bend their arm over your thigh (**Figure 18**). Turn your body and move your foot to the other side of your partner's head. At this point your partner's arm should be clamped between your chest and thigh (**Figure 19**).

Figure 18

Figure 19

Sit up in order to lock your partner's shoulder joint (**Figure 20**). Sit back and deliver a controlled hammer-fist strike to the base of the opponent's skull (**Figure 21**).

Figure 20

Figure 21

Transition Drill 2

This drill contains a few arm-locks not covered in the previous drill. Your partner grabs your clothing. Cover your partner's hand, step backward and use your forearm to strike the inside of your partner's forearm. This strike will turn the opponent's head and throw their shoulder backward (**Figure 22**). Raise your arm and deliver a controlled forearm strike to the underside of your partner's jaw (**Figure 23**). The first part of this drill is one of the applications of the 'rising block'. Bring your striking hand back and grab your partner's hand (**Figure 24**).Bring your lead foot back, turn your body and use your elbow to push against their

Figure 22

Figure 23

Figure 24

elbow. This will lock your partner's arm and cause them to bend at the waist (**Figure 25**). Maintain your grip on your partner's hand and ensure that their wrist is bent with their fingers pointing upward. Place your other hand on the inside of your partner's elbow joint (**Figure 26**). Pivot on your foot and turn your body so that you are square on to your partner. As you turn, rotate your partner's hand, so that their fingers move towards them, and pull your partner's elbow towards you. This motion will bend your partner's arm and rotate the bones of their forearm together. This lock will drop your partner to their knees (**Figure 27**). Deliver a knee strike (**Figure 28**).

Figure 25

Figure 26

Figure 27

Figure 28

Pivot on your foot, grab your partner's wrist and use your free hand to push against their elbow joint. This will position your partner for the following strike (**Figure 29**). Maintain a tight hold on your partner's wrist and deliver a controlled heel of palm strike to their skull (**Figure 30**). Place your striking hand back onto your partner's elbow and move forwards in order to force them onto the floor (**Figure 31**).

Figure 29

Figure 30

Figure 31

Push down on your partner's elbow and pull up on their wrist to lock the arm (**Figure 32**). As soon as your partner taps, fold your partner's arm around your own arm and lock your partner's shoulder (**Figure 33**). Deliver a controlled hammer-fist strike before regaining an upright position (**Figure 34**).

Figure 32

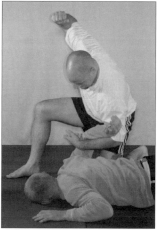

Figure 33

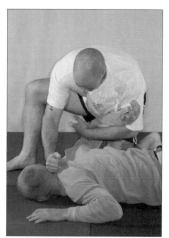

Figure 34

Transition Drill 3

The final drill we will look at is constructed entirely of techniques which are either taken directly from the Pinan / Heian series, or are based on principles found in that series. It is shown here for the two ground fighting arm-locks that appear towards the end of the drill and to give an example of a drill which includes the integrated use of a variety methods. Your partner reaches forwards and attempts to grab your chest (**Figure 35**). Push their arm across and shift to a forty-five degree angle. The non-pushing arm should be positioned above your partner's arm (**Figure 36**). Wrap your arm around your partner's arm, pull them towards you and deliver a forearm strike to the base of their skull (**Figure 37**).

Figure 35

Figure 36

Figure 37

Figure 38

The first part of this drill is an application of the forty-five degree 'knife-hand blocks' found in Pinan Shodan (Heian Nidan). Maintain your grip on your partner's arm and deliver an elbow strike to the side of their jaw. This elbowing technique is found in Pinan / Heian Godan (**Figure 38**). Turn your body and secure the opponent in a headlock. This headlock and the following throw are found in Pinan / Heian Sandan (**Figure 39**). Keep a tight grip on the opponent's arm and head. Step forward and push your hips backward so that they block the path of your partner's legs. Execute a cross-buttocks throw to take your partner over the back of your hips. For more information on this throw see my book *Throws for Strikers* (**Figure 40**). This throw is often mislabelled as a 'forearm block'. Maintain your grip on the opponent's head and arm so that you land in the scarf-hold (**Figure 41**).

Figure 39

Figure 40

Figure 41

In practise you need to be careful and perform the throw gently so that you don't land on your partner. Secure a grip on your partner's wrist and swap the position of your legs. Bar your partner's arm over your thigh (**Figure 42**). Barring an opponent's arm over your thigh appears in Pinan Nidan kata (use of 'short cat stance'). Return your legs to the initial position, extend your lead leg and push your partner's arm down over your thigh (**Figure 43**). Place your shin over your partner's forearm.

Figure 42

Figure 43

Hook your foot behind the knee of your other leg and roll
forward to twist your partner's shoulder joint (**Figure** 44). This
lock exploits the same limitations and employs the same
principles as the opening lock of Pinan Shodan (Heian Nidan)
kata. Drop back and deliver a controlled strike to your partner's
face to complete the drill (**Figure** 45).

Figure 44

Figure 45

That concludes the transition drills covered in this book. You can learn more about these and other drills by watching my *Combat Drills* video. It is important that you understand that these drills are just drills. It is certainly not the intention that in a live fight you would utilise every single technique in the order presented in the drill! The intention is to help you to learn to flow from one technique to the next and to see the opportunities that the techniques create and how those opportunities can be exploited.

It should be remembered that in live situations you should always try to assure your safety as soon as possible. You should never move on to apply further techniques when you could be fleeing. I'll stress again that these are practise drills, not 'combinations' to be employed in a live fight. It should also be understood that these drills, useful though they are, are not a substitute for live non-compliant sparring.

You are encouraged to adapt these drills to meet your own needs and to come up with transition drills of your own. The key thing to ensure is that all the transitions in the drill exploit the opportunities created by the previous technique. It is also important to ensure that you maintain dominance over the opponent and never give them the chance to recompose themselves.

Conclusion

Although knowledge of arm-locks is essential if you are to be a rounded martial artist, it is important to remember that arm-locks are definitely not primary techniques in live situations. Arm-locks are techniques of opportunity. They can certainly be used effectively if the ideal opportunity arises, but we should not be seeking to apply arm-locks in the first instance.

It should always be remembered that arm-locks are support techniques and that other more direct techniques should be your first choice. That said, arm-locks should not be slighted as they can be very effective, providing they are used in the right situation, in the right way and at the right time.

In order to get arm-locks to work for you it is vital that you get plenty of practise. Reading about arm-locks won't give you the ability to apply them. Only practising applying arm-locks will give you the ability to apply arm-locks.

To begin with, you should practise the techniques in isolation until you are confident with the mechanics of the movement. You should then practise drilling the techniques in a more flowing way and develop your ability to move quickly from one technique to the next. Once basic competence has been achieved, you should then integrate the techniques into your live practise.

In addition to looking at how to perform the locks themselves, we have also covered the core principles associated with all arm-locks. It is absolutely vital that you gain a pragmatic understanding of these principles. There are many other arm-locks in addition to those covered in this book. However, you should remember that all arm-locks are based on the same core principles that we discussed in Chapter One. Once you understand these principles, you will see that all the differing arm-locks are essentially just variations on common themes. You are encouraged to build upon the techniques and principles shown in this book and to further expand your knowledge of arm-locks.

I'd like to finish by thanking you for purchasing this book and taking the time to read it. If it was not for your support, and the support of my other readers, I wouldn't have anyone to write for! And that would be a shame as I find writing a lot of fun. Thanks once again for your support. It is hugely appreciated.

Iain Abernethy

Back row left to right:
Murray Denwood, Paul Cartmell, Peter Skillen (photographer),
Iain Abernethy (author), Fred Moore, Gary Herbert,
Front Row: Jim Hopkins, Craig Strickland.

Books & Videos

Throws for Strikers (see page 146)

'*Throws for Strikers: The Forgotten Throws of Karate, Boxing & Taekwondo*' looks at the basic throws that were once commonly practised in striking systems such as Karate, Boxing and Taekwondo. In addition to providing instruction on the throws themselves, this book also covers the fundamental principles that apply to all throws, practise drills that will enable the reader to develop competence in live situations, and what to do should a throw go wrong and you end up on the ground. '*Throws for Strikers*' also reveals where throws are recorded in the traditional forms (Katas / Hyungs) and discusses how throws were used in the bare-knuckle boxing matches of old. This book will enable practitioners of striking systems to reintroduce the basic throwing methods that were once part of their art.

"Iain Abernethy is building up an impressive body of work. This compact, well presented and technique heavy volume will only add to his growing reputation" - Traditional Karate Magazine

ISBN 0-9538932-2-7
240 x 170 mm
96 pages
120 Illustrations
£9.99 Paperback
Available from all good bookstores or direct from NETH Publishing
United Kingdom + £1.00 UK P&P
Rep. of Ireland & Europe + £2.50 P&P
Rest of the World + £4.00 P&P

Bunkai-Jutsu:
The Practical Application of Karate Kata

'*Bunkai-Jutsu*' is the analysis of the karate katas and their application in real combat. It is also the title of this pioneering book by Iain Abernethy. The fighting

applications of the karate katas (forms) is one of the most fascinating – and sadly misunderstood – aspects of karate practise. Bunkai-Jutsu provides the reader with the information they need to unlock the 'secrets' of kata and to begin practising karate as the complete and realistic combat art that it was intended to be! This groundbreaking and often controversial book provides a detailed analysis of the combative concepts and principles upon which the katas are based. This book is essential reading for all those who want to understand the real meaning of kata.

"Bunkai-Jutsu explains every aspect of the katas and their application in real combat" – Doug James 7th Dan

"No martial arts library is complete without Bunkai-Jutsu. Iain Abernethy has shown us the real beauty of karate."
– Geoff Thompson, self-protection expert and best-selling author.

ISBN 0-9538932-1-9
246 x 189 mm
240 pages
Over 235 Illustrations
£17.99 Paperback
Available from all good bookstores or direct from NETH Publishing
United Kingdom + £3.01 UK P&P
Rep. of Ireland & Europe + £4.51 P&P
Rest of the World + £6.01 P&P

Karate's Grappling Methods

This heavily illustrated book takes a detailed look at the grappling techniques of karate. Topics covered include: understanding kata and bunkai, the role of grappling in self-defence, close-range strikes, throws and takedowns, ground-fighting holds, chokes and strangles, arm-bars, leg and ankle locks, neck-wrenches, finger-locks, wrist-locks, fighting dirty?, combinations and live grappling drills.

"At long last, a credible and marvellous book on the application of Karate kata! And not one that skims the surface looking for frills and thrills, succeeding to entertain but failing abysmally to prepare one for a real, in your face encounter. Rather this book is an in-depth, thoughtful and thought-provoking examination of possibly the deadliest of arts. Karate's Grappling Methods is a great and inspired book." – Geoff Thompson.

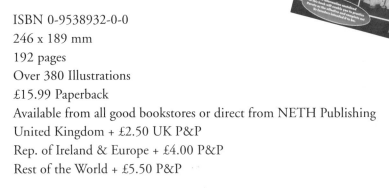

ISBN 0-9538932-0-0
246 x 189 mm
192 pages
Over 380 Illustrations
£15.99 Paperback
Available from all good bookstores or direct from NETH Publishing
United Kingdom + £2.50 UK P&P
Rep. of Ireland & Europe + £4.00 P&P
Rest of the World + £5.50 P&P

Combat Drills: from Form to Function

This video presents 20 two-person combat drills which are designed to cover all ranges of fighting in a fluid and pragmatic way. These drills cover a variety of strikes, throws, chokes, takedowns, arm-locks, neck-cranks, strangles, leg-locks, holds and ground-fighting techniques.

These drills are suitable for all martial artists who understand the importance of possessing skills at all ranges and the need to be able to flow from one technique to the next whilst maintaining dominance over an opponent.

The 20 drills shown on this tape include numerous applications from many different katas (forms). For those martial artists who practice forms, these drills will aid in the progression from *Form* to combative *Function* and may be used as an alternative to classical one-step practise.

"*Once again, Abernethy breaks down the barriers between the traditional and the modern and presents a flowing series of techniques across all ranges*" - Traditional Karate Magazine

"*Martial artists that may previously have thought that a 'static' traditional art can offer them nothing new, especially in the 'pavement arena' could do far worse than to give Abernethy a go, as his flowing range of techniques, enthusiasm and no nonsense approach may change (and open) your mind*"
- Combat Magazine

Running Time: approx. 1 Hour 10 Mins
£19.45 inc. UK Postage & Packing
Rep. of Ireland & Europe +£1.50
Rest of the World +£3.00

Bunkai-Jutsu: Practical Kata Applications
Volume 1: The Pinan / Heian Series

'Bunkai-Jutsu' is the analysis of the karate katas and their application in real combat. These high-quality tapes reveal the effective fighting applications recorded in the katas. The application of every single move is shown complete with instruction on the style variations. These videos are a must for all karateka – regardless of style – who wish to practise karate as a complete and effective combat system.

Volume one covers the applications of the Pinan / Heian (peaceful mind) series. The great Anko Itosu formulated these katas in the early 1900s. They are a complete system of fighting in their own right and were designed to be a collection of the most effective methods being practised in the Shuri region of Okinawa at that time. This video examines the strikes, locks, throws, chokes, strangles, traps, ground-fighting and combative strategies recorded within the Pinan / Heian series.

Running Time: approx. 2 Hours
£19.45 inc. UK Postage & Packing
Rep. of Ireland & Europe +£1.50
Rest of the World +£3.00

Bunkai-Jutsu: Practical Kata Applications
Volume 2: Naihanchi / Tekki & Bassai

'*Bunkai-Jutsu*' is the analysis of the karate katas and their application in real combat. These high-quality tapes reveal the effective fighting applications recorded in the katas. The application of every single move is shown complete with instruction on the style variations. These videos are a must for all karateka – regardless of style – who wish to practise karate as a complete and effective combat system.

Volume two covers Naihanchi (Tekki) and Bassai-Dai (Passai). Today, Naihanchi / Tekki is often undervalued due to its simplistic appearance. This video shows the highly effective close-range fighting applications of the form and reveals just why the kata was so highly regarded by the masters of old. The second part of the tape covers Passai / Bassai-Dai kata and demonstrates the strikes, throws, takedowns, locks, neck-cranks, chokes, combative strategies etc that have made this form one of the most popular in the history of karate.

"*Abernethy imparts a great deal of knowledge fluently, discussing the reason for each turn or movement in great detail, not only explaining the practical effectiveness of the techniques but also the defining principles behind them. Thus, through repetition, reinforcement and lucid narration, he once again demonstrates that effective self defence can be found within Karate ... As with Volume One, this is real value for money, wall to wall technique from a man who obviously has a real passion for his karate, and at a time when self-defence concerns are prevalent, he proves that this traditional art can cut it as a modern fighting system*"
– Traditional Karate Magazine

Running Time: approx. 1 Hour 30 Mins
£19.45 inc. UK Postage & Packing
Rep. of Ireland & Europe +£1.50
Rest of the World +£3.00

Bunkai-Jutsu: Practical Kata Applications
Volume 3: Kushanku / Kanku-Dai

'*Bunkai-Jutsu*' is the analysis of the karate katas and their application in real combat. These high-quality tapes reveal the effective fighting applications recorded in the katas. The application of every single move is shown complete with instruction on the style variations. These videos are a must for all karateka – regardless of style – who wish to practise karate as a complete and effective combat system.

Volume 3 covers the applications of Kushanku / Kanku-Dai. The kata is a record of the highly effective striking and grappling methods taught by the Chinese martial artist *Kushanku*. It is said that the kata was constructed by the legendary *Tode Sakagawa*, who became a student of *Kushanku's* when he came to Okinawa in 1756. This kata is also known as Kosokun (alternative pronunciation) and Kanku-Dai (Japanese name for the form). This video provides instruction on the no-nonsense fighting techniques recorded within the kata.

"*Abernethy continues to bring the lesser known and varied applications of the traditional kata to a wider audience, fusing the traditional and modern to create a series of tapes with genuine relevance to contemporary self-defence issues. Bunkai-Jutsu Volume 3 looks at the practical applications of Kushanku / Kanku-Dai Kata, breaking it down into each individual move and then dissecting its practical application with authority and ingenuity; providing a wealth of techniques and variations*"
- Combat Magazine

Running Time: approx. 1 Hour 30 Mins
£19.45 inc. UK Postage & Packing
Rep. of Ireland & Europe +£1.50
Rest of the World +£3.00

Karate's Grappling Methods

See the Karate katas brought to life with these professionally produced videos. Both videos provide in-depth instruction on the highly effective close-range techniques and concepts recorded within the karate katas. Related methods from other arts are also covered.

(The KGM book and Videos contain many differing techniques in addition to supporting one another)

Karate's Grappling Methods: Volume 1

- Close-Range Strikes
- Neck-Cranks
- Arm-Locks
- Wrist-Locks
- Leg-Locks

Running Time: approx. 50 minutes
£16.50 inc. UK Postage & Packing
Rep. of Ireland & Europe +£1.50
Rest of the World +£3.00

Karate's Grappling Methods: Volume 2

- Throws & Takedowns
- Chokes & Strangles
- Finger-Locks
- Ground-Fighting Holds
- Keeping it Simple
- Nerve Points
- Live Sparring.

Running Time: approx. 50 minutes
£16.50 inc. UK Postage & Packing
Rep. of Ireland & Europe +£1.50
Rest of the World +£3.00

Ordering and Contact Details

By Post to:
NETH Publishing, PO Box 38, Cockermouth,
Cumbria, CA13 0GS, United Kingdom.

Please make Cheques / UK Postal Orders payable to
"NETH Publishing"

24hr Credit / Debit Card Hot-line:
01900829406 (United Kingdom)
+44 1900829406 (International)

Website:
Order on-line at www.iainabernethy.com

For a full list of all NETH Publishing products,
please send your name and address to NETH
Publishing.

Iain Abernethy can be contacted via the NETH
Publishing address or e-mailed at:
iain@iainabernethy.com

www.iainabernethy.com

www.summersdale.com

Introduction to Throws for Strikers

In recent times, more and more martial artists are critically reevaluating the effectiveness of their chosen art. The need for skills at all ranges of combat is now more widely understood. You could be the best kicker in the world, but if you don't know how to grapple you will be easily defeated if your opponent gets inside kicking range (which isn't that hard to do). Also, just suppose that you're a great wrestler, but have had no exposure to striking. It may take you longer to defeat an opponent (strikes being a quicker way to end fights), you will be very vulnerable to strikes and, most importantly of all, you will not have the ability to 'stun and run', which is vital for effective self-protection.

A chain is only as strong as its weakest link. To be a truly effective fighter, you will need to be conversant with all ranges of combat. This realisation has led to strikers learning how to grapple and grapplers learning to strike. However, one question that needs to be asked is, 'why doesn't the art you already practise have those missing skills on its curriculum?' If the original martial arts were designed for use in real combat, then why are there such glaring omissions?

Over the last century, the martial arts have undergone many significant changes. Most important of all has been a fundamental change to the goals of training. The original goal of all the martial arts was the defeat of an opponent in military or civilian combat, but the focus of many systems has now changed. Most practitioners of the martial arts, whether they realise it or not, now train for physical development or sport.

For the practitioner who trains in the martial arts to stay in shape, it does not really matter if all ranges of combat are practised. All that is needed is for the training to be physically taxing enough to improve their level of fitness. Likewise, if the same practitioner has the necessary muscle control, flexibility and physical strength to perform the various physical movements, katas, forms, prearranged techniques etc, it is irrelevant whether they have the skill to actually apply those movements in live combat. In today's martial arts, mastery of physical movement is often all that is required to advance through the grades. Hence, we have the situation where many higher grades, though technically competent, are not actually able to apply what they have learnt in live situations.

The other modern trend in the martial arts is the shift towards sport. In this instance, the goal is the acquisition of trophies and titles through the defeat of practitioners of the same discipline in a rule bound environment. This evolution has seen those techniques that are not associated with sporting success fall by the wayside. Karate, boxing, taekwondo etc have always favoured striking methods, and that is why their sporting versions have evolved into solely striking affairs. Judo, on the other hand, has always favoured grappling. Judo did originally contain striking techniques. However, the rules of competitive judo prohibit striking; hence you would now find it fairly difficult to find a judo club that teaches striking. The older versions of karate and taekwondo contained throws, joint-locks, strangles etc. Again, many of these techniques are now banned in the modern sporting versions of karate and taekwondo, and therefore very few schools now teach the grappling side of those arts.

Not only do these modern evolutions limit the techniques available to the art's practitioners, they also increase their vulnerabilities. For example, because wrestlers never have to face kicks and punches in a competitive bout, they are never exposed to strikes and are therefore unlikely to be able to deal with them effectively. Conversely, the modern boxer will be highly skilled at dealing with punches, but will be vulnerable to kicks, throws etc.

The original fighting arts were for use in real combat, and therefore they covered all ranges. The karateka of the past covered throwing, grappling, locking etc in their training (see my books, *Karate's Grappling Methods* and *Bunkai-Jutsu: The Practical Application of Karate Kata*). So did boxers, kung-fu stylists and practitioners of what became known as taekwondo. A quick look through the history books, and an examination of the traditional forms, reveals grappling techniques in abundance.

Karate was strongly influenced by many differing styles of Chinese boxing. This included the methods of Shuai Jiao (a form of Chinese wrestling that is said to date back to 2000 BC) and Chin-Na (seizing and joint locking). Karate has also been influenced by the native Okinawan grappling art of Tegumi and, to a lesser degree, the Aiki-Jujitsu systems of the Japanese samurai.

Boxing also used to contain many grappling and throwing techniques. It is believed that modern boxing (and wrestling) evolved from the Greek art of Pankration (meaning 'all powerful'). This art contained strikes, holds, throws, ground-fighting and submissions. Greek mythology states that both Hercules and Theseus were skilled in the art of Pankration.

In more recent times, there is an abundance of records that refer to boxers using grappling and throwing techniques. As an example, James Figg – who was the first ever bare-knuckle boxing champion of England – defended his title against Ned Sutton in 1727. It is recorded that Figg winded Sutton by throwing him on his back, and that Figg eventually won the bout by knocking Sutton down and pinning him until he submitted! These techniques are now never seen in the modern sport of boxing. However, they were a part of the original system. Boxing was taught as a self-defence system to society gentlemen. The first gloves were developed so that they could practise the art without picking up bumps and bruises that were not befitting their status. Throwing was also considered to be an important part of the self-defence side of boxing.

Taekwondo is a relatively modern art; the name 'taekwondo' first being used in 1955. However, it is said that its origins go back much further. Taekwondo is based on the warrior art of Tae Kyon, which was formulated by the warriors of the Koguryo kingdom and was then spread to the whole of Korea by the Hwarang (warrior class) of the Silla kingdom. The Korean arts of Subak, Kwonbop and Cireum (a wrestling art based on Chinese and Mongolian systems) are also said to have influenced the development of what became taekwondo. Chinese kempo and in particular Okinawan and Japanese karate have also influenced modern taekwondo. Indeed, many of the original taekwondo forms were based on the karate katas. These 'common forms' mean that taekwondo will also have been influenced by Okinawan and Japanese grappling and throwing techniques. Whilst grappling is not a commonly practised part of the art today, we can see that grappling techniques were a part of the systems upon which the modern art of taekwondo is based.

Although many styles of Kung-fu are now practised as striking only systems, wrestling and joint-locking are traditionally regarded as a standard part of all Chinese martial arts. Traditional kung-fu is said to be made up of four sections; Striking, kicking, wrestling and joint-locks. We have already discussed how the methods of Chinese wrestling have influenced karate and taekwondo. The Japanese methods of jujitsu (upon which modern judo is based) were also influenced by Chinese grappling methods. As with karate and taekwondo, a study of the traditional forms will often reveal many grappling and throwing techniques.

Not only did the striking arts originally contain grappling and throwing techniques, grappling arts such as wrestling, judo, aikido etc also originally contained striking techniques. It is only in relatively recent times that the martial arts have narrowed their focus. However, this narrowing of focus has had a positive side. Because the vast majority of boxers have now abandoned the grappling side of their art to concentrate solely on punching, they have become exceptional punchers. Judoka are without a doubt the premier throwers of the martial arts community due to the heavy emphasis that they now place on throwing.

The original arts, although much more broad based, were not as sophisticated as their modern counterparts. The modern practitioners of the various arts have taken certain aspects to levels never dreamed of by their predecessors, and this has benefited the martial arts as a whole. However, some aspects of these increased levels of sophistication can bring their own problems, which we will discuss in the following chapter.

It must also be understood that communication was very limited during the times our arts were being developed. Today, it is possible to learn many arts from all over the world. In the past, however, people would only be able to study with practitioners who lived in their local area. For example, the boxers of England would not have been able to study with the jujitsu practitioners of Japan. This is one more reason why the techniques of the older arts are not always as sophisticated as those we have access to today. This lack of sophistication does not mean these techniques are ineffective, far from it. However, it must be said that the 'forgotten' aspects of the older arts are often not as refined as the techniques of those arts now dedicated to particular skills (as you would expect).

If effective fighting skills are your aim, then you need to include all ranges of combat in your training. There are essentially two ways to ensure that your training is broad based. The first is to study a variety of arts ('cross-training' as it is often called). For example, you may study boxing for your punches, taekwondo for your kicking, and judo for your grappling. This is obviously a great way to train because you are effectively learning the strongest aspects of the various arts. The downside is that you may become a 'jack of all trades and a master of none'. And unless you get sufficient guidance from experienced cross-trainers, the various methods can become disjointed with none of the systems being practised gelling together.

The second way to ensure your training is broad based is to study the older version of your current art. The advantage of this approach is that you will be learning a single complete and coherent system. The negative side is that the methods of the older version of your art will often not be as sophisticated or refined as those of the dedicated grappling arts. If you're a boxer, you could learn the throws that were once a fundamental part of boxing. If you're a karate, taekwondo or kung-fu practitioner, you could examine the grappling techniques that are recorded within the traditional forms. You should understand that studying the throwing techniques of the striking arts will in no way make you the equal of a judoka or wrestler when it comes to throws. However, a study of the 'forgotten' throws will give you the fundamental throwing skills that may be needed for self-protection. It's really a matter of what you as an individual require from your training.

My personal approach has been to fully study my chosen art (karate), and to examine the methods of dedicated grappling arts to increase my understanding of the techniques and concepts already present in my base system. However, as I said, it's really a matter of what works best for you. Some of my training partners and students also study judo, which has not only enhanced their application of the basic throwing techniques found within the traditional forms, but it has also furthered their knowledge and understanding of throwing techniques in general.

There are many different aspects to grappling. In this book we will be concentrating on the throws and takedowns that were once a common part of the striking arts. Differing arts may have emphasised certain throws over others, or have performed them in slightly differing ways to those shown here. However, the throws shown in this book are common to many arts (grappling and striking) and, in my opinion, are some of the most effective throws for use in self-defence. Exploring all the throws originally found in what are now called the 'striking systems' would be a huge task. It is hoped that the throws covered in this book will help you to further explore the specific throws found within your own system. You may not perform the throws covered in exactly the same way as demonstrated, but the fundamental concepts are common to all systems. What works, works!

The purpose of this book is to help practitioners of the striking arts to reintroduce the throwing methods that were once part of their system. This will then allow you to practise your art as its founders originally intended. These throws can obviously also be found in the grappling systems and we will make reference to these arts where appropriate.